Y0-BRC-833

Legal Writing
The Strategy of Persuasion

Third Edition

Norman Brand
John O. White

St. Martin's Press
New York

Editor: Edward Hutchinson
Manager, publishing services: Emily Berleth
Publishing services associate: Kalea Chapman
Project management: Omega Publishing Services, Inc.
Art director: Sheree Goodman
Cover design: Levavi & Levavi

Library of Congress Catalog Card Number: 92-62765

For information, write:
St. Martin's Press, Inc.
175 Fifth Avenue
New York, NY 10010

ISBN: 0-312-08972-4

About the Authors

Norman Brand, Ph.D., J.D., has taught English, legal writing, and labor law. He began teaching legal writing for the Council on Legal Education Opportunity in 1968, and served as their Consultant in Writing through 1974. He designed and taught the first undergraduate legal writing course in the country, at the University of California, Davis, in 1973. From 1980 through 1985, while a professor at Albany Law School, he served as the Chair of the Association of American Law Schools' Section on Legal Writing, Reasoning, and Research. He was a member of the Advisory Board of the Document Design Center's project on Clear and Effective Legal Writing, and a member of the American Bar Association's Committee on Legal Writing. He has taught legal writing at the National Judicial College, and lectured on the subject for the Federal Administrative Law Judge's Conference, the American College of Probate Counsel, the Practising Law Institute, the American Arbitration Association, and other organizations. He is currently engaged in the full-time practice of alternative dispute resolution.

Dr. John O. White, Professor of English at California State University, Fullerton, has taught legal writing in a number of programs for over twenty years. He developed and has taught an undergraduate course in legal writing at CSUF as well as regular legal writing workshops at Western State University College of Law. For several years, he also taught Language and Legal Analysis at the University of Southern California School of Law. In addition, Dr. White taught as legal writing professor for the Council on Legal Education Opportunity at the University of Washington Law School. Besides teaching English and legal writing, he is also active as a consultant in the assessment of writing skills for the Educational Testing Service, the California Department of Justice, and other organizations.

Preface

The third edition of *Legal Writing: The Strategy of Persuasion* has been written to help law and pre-law students in several ways. First, it is designed to be used as a primary or supplementary textbook in law school courses in legal writing and legal analysis. To that end, it focuses on law examinations, legal memoranda, and legal briefs. Second, the book may be used in undergraduate, pre-law courses in legal writing. For pre-law as well as law students, we have presumed no particular legal background. All examples and writing exercises provide simplified rules of law that can be applied to hypothetical situations. Third, we have written this text so that it may be used by law students and pre-law students as a self-contained guide to the process of writing the kinds of assignments required in law school. Students who want to get a head start on law school, or who want to improve their writing ability before their first law exam, will find specific writing strategies and tactics in this book. Finally, the textbook has also been found to be a valuable resource in a number of paralegal preparation programs.

Law professors and writing instructors who have used *Legal Writing* in past years will be glad to see that the third edition has retained the familiar and valuable features of the first two editions and has added new materials and chapters to make it even more useful.

Chapter One, THE PROCESS OF LEGAL WRITING, is an analysis of the rhetoric of persuasion and the writing process as they apply to legal writing. In this chapter, we examine the pre-writing considerations of purpose, audience, and form, and take the student through the separate writing steps involved in composing and revising. We give the student practical answers to the questions, "How do I get started?" and, "What do I do next?"

In Chapter Two, THE STRATEGY OF LEGAL PERSUASION, we analyze the tasks called for in writing an answer to a law examination question. Then, we present writing strategies and techniques necessary to produce a successful answer.

In Chapter Three, WRITING AN ANSWER TO A LAW EXAMINATION, we take the reader step-by-step through the process of analysis and writing using a sample law examination question. While there is no "trick" to answering a law question, no panacea that will ensure superior grades, we demonstrate a practical approach that enables students to analyze a problem, spot the issues, and organize an answer logically and effectively.

The next two chapters expand upon the second edition's Chapter Four to give more comprehensive coverage of writing memoranda and briefs. Chapter Four, WRITING LEGAL MEMORANDA, presents a careful and detailed analysis of requirements and techniques for writing legal memoranda. We explain their purpose, audience, and format, and offer suggestions for thoughtful analysis, clear organization, and appropriate style. We also provide specific writing strategies and models for the writer. Finally, we provide real world examples, new to this edition, of an intraoffice memorandum and a memorandum of points and authorities.

Chapter Five, WRITING LEGAL BRIEFS, is an analysis of the process for writing legal briefs. We emphasize format and audience, and offer strategies and techniques for writing effective legal briefs. In a new addition to the third edition, we also include a legal brief that was successful in the U.S. Supreme Court.

In Chapter Six, LOGIC AND ARGUMENT, we examine the underlying logic of persuasive legal writing. We explain the terms "logical argument," and "law structured argument," to help students understand the conceptual framework of their writing. We also examine and discuss the skills of recognizing and using slanted language.

Chapter Seven, THE MECHANICS OF LEGAL WRITING, provides a review of common mechanical and grammatical problems that occur in legal writing. We analyze the problems and suggest ways students can identify and correct their errors.

In Chapter Eight, LEGAL WRITING STYLE, we analyze the nature of writing style and present approaches that help students eliminate stylistic flaws. One of our major goals in this chapter is to try to simplify and clarify legal writing style. It is an antidote to the disease of "legalese," which often blights law student writing.

Chapter Nine, SAMPLE PROBLEMS AND ANSWERS, contains law examination questions with representative and complete sample answers.

Finally, in a new Appendix, we offer a number of writing exercises—hypothetical law questions—so students can practice their writing.

Together, these chapters provide students with a comprehensive and analytical look at the kind of writing required in law school along with strategies and techniques for achieving success on those writing assignments.

Any student who is in law school, or who plans to go to law school, may study this textbook for a detailed analysis of exactly what is expected in law school assignments. It will provide students with writing strategies that will enable them to write successful briefs, memoranda, and answers to law examination questions.

Acknowledgments

We are indebted to our students, to our faculty colleagues, and to all of those who used the first two editions of this book for their suggestions and encouragement. We are especially grateful to Terence Collins, University of Minnesota; Mary Sue Donsky, Esq., Long Island University; Susan Griffin, The UCLA Writing Programs; Ronald Newman, University of Miami; Kellis Parker, University of California, Davis, School of Law; Richard Reynolds, University of Connecticut; David R. Samuelson, Southwestern University School of Law; Robert N. St. Clair, University of Louisville; Barry Vickrey, University of North Dakota School of Law; Rachel Vorspan, Fordham Law School; Michael Werth, formerly of University of Maryland; Marilyn Williams, Johnson County Community College; and Richard Wydick, University of California, Davis, School of Law. We also wish to thank George W. White for the graphics. Special thanks go to Alan Berkowitz, Peter Nussbaum, and Marsha S. Berzon for contributing materials to this edition.

Contents

CHAPTER ONE
The Process
of Legal Writing

INTRODUCTION

Most expository writing, and certainly most that is required in law school, is persuasive writing. Writers try to persuade their readers to do something, buy something, or believe something. The rhetoric of persuasion may take any of several different forms in writing, from emotional appeals to subliminal suggestions and from intricate logical constructions to inferential leaps. And advertising, evangelism, and politics may employ some of these strategies of persuasion when they are appropriate to their audiences and purposes. The strategy of persuasion appropriate for legal writing, however, requires concise, clear, complete, and logical explanation and argument. It requires a clear statement of issue, a complete discussion of relevant factors, and a logical analysis of points leading to a conclusion. Finally, legal writing requires clear, concise, and plain language.

Our goal in this textbook is to help you understand the writing process that results in good legal writing. The law exam answer, memo, or brief that you turn in is the result of a process involving many separate but interrelated stages. We will go through those steps, examining, explaining, and illustrating the process.

LEGAL WRITING

A law student has three major kinds of writing assignments: the law examination, the legal memorandum, and the legal brief.

The Law Exam

Most law examinations present a hypothetical fact situation and call for analysis and a conclusion.

A throws a rock at B that hits C. B, in dodging the rock, knocks D off the curb, breaking D's leg.
Discuss the rights and liabilities of all the parties.

In keeping with the instructor's directions (or "call of the question"), you must analyze the situation, identify the legal issues, apply the rules of law, and conjecture on the outcome of any possible legal action. But what is most critical is that your reasoning process be clearly shown and your conclusions be supported by fact and discussion. While specific methods for answering this type of question are discussed in later chapters, the important thing to remember here is that the law exam is graded on the basis of the argument, the analysis, and the reasoning—not merely the conclusion.

Legal Memoranda

Intraoffice Memorandum.   A legal memorandum, also called an intraoffice memorandum or simply an office memo, while requiring similar analytical abilities, is a researched and objective discussion of a hypothetical—and usually complex—fact situation.

During a security check at the boarding gate of an airline, an employee of the Smith Detective Agency noticed a white powder in the bottom of Walter's briefcase. The employee called a deputy sheriff who was standing nearby and showed him what he had found. The deputy told Walter he would have to search him. Walter objected to the search, but the deputy patted him down.

The deputy felt a soft object in Walter's inside coat pocket and demanded that Walter show him what was in the pocket. Walter refused. The deputy then reached into Walter's pocket and pulled out what appeared to be a packet of cocaine.

Walter was arrested and charged with possession of cocaine. Upon analysis, the powder in the briefcase turned out to be talcum powder, but the packet did contain cocaine. At the trial the cocaine was introduced into evidence over Walter's objection. Walter was convicted of possession of cocaine and sentenced to six months in jail.

You are to write a memorandum to the senior partner in your firm, discussing whether Walter should appeal his conviction.

Memorandum of Points and Authorities. While called a memorandum, this document more closely resembles a legal brief. Instead of an objective analysis, the memorandum of points and authorities is like a minibrief filed in support of a motion. It provides case references and argument in support of a conclusion.

The Legal Brief

A brief is a complete formal presentation of an argument for a plaintiff or defendant. In the brief, a law student may be assigned either side. For example, a student may be asked to write a legal brief presenting Walter's side in the case given above. Writing a brief requires skillful persuasion and the ability to make clear the reasoning behind the position.

(A brief should not be confused with "briefing" a case. To brief a case is to make specific notes on a case in order to remember the key elements. It is really just a matter of taking notes following an accepted format in preparing an individual study guide.)

We will discuss each kind of writing assignment in more detail in the following chapters, but for now you should remember that writing skills for all of these assignments are based on similar principles and strategies of persuasive writing. A general overview of the writing process involved should prepare you for the specific task of writing answers to law questions, legal memoranda, and briefs.

THE WRITING PROCESS

Struggling writers might like to imagine that others—natural writers—somehow find writing easy. They might like to think that those lucky few are gifted with an ability to sit down and immediately write a polished draft. Divine intervention or inspiration must account for that clear and lucid prose.

The truth is that writing is not easy, and a skilled writer has developed his or her talent by mastering a process that leads to a clear, well-organized, detailed final draft. The process is not the same for every writer. We all begin, stop, make progress, stop, and begin again. Thus, the process is sometimes recursive rather than direct. We can, however, identify three distinct stages in the writing process: pre-writing/planning, writing/drafting, and revising/editing.

Pre-Writing

Most students who have problems in writing spend too little time in the first, pre-writing stage. They begin to draft before they are clear about what they intend to say and about what strategies and steps they mean to use. These students know only where they are to start and roughly where they intend to arrive. Too often they end up somewhere else. Even if they do arrive at the planned destination, they may have traveled a circuitous and rocky path to get there. There is a better way.

Before beginning to draft, you must be clear about audience and purpose. You must have analyzed the problem, established a solution, and developed a strategy for explaining that solution. You must have anticipated problems and counterarguments. And you must have organized your ideas so that you know where you are going before beginning to write. Working out these issues properly takes place during the pre-writing/planning phase.

Purpose.   The first consideration in pre-writing is understanding the purpose of the writing assignment. In a law examination you may be asked to discuss and decide all issues, or to discuss the rights and liabilities of all the parties, or to address particular issues. Those writing instructions are sometimes referred to as "the call of the question," and they establish your immediate task. There is, however, more to purpose than the call of the question. You must think of the writing assignment as the place you demonstrate the clarity of your thinking, your skill in analysis, your ability to explain, your logical reasoning, and your clear and effective writing. The purpose of a law examination, memo, or legal brief assignment is not only to determine if you can arrive at a right answer, it is to test your ability to analyze, synthesize, organize, and explain the law. When you understand that you have to do much more than come up with the "right" answer, you can begin to plan a successful response to a legal writing assignment.

Audience. At first glance, the question of audience may appear to have a simple answer: your law professor or writing instructor is your audience. But to understand the importance of audience in your writing, you need to ask a few more questions and clarify your assumptions. It is true that you are writing for your instructor, the one who will evaluate your work. What is it about your audience that will help prepare you to write? What will your audience be looking for? What will appeal to the reader? What is expected of you?

If, when you think of an audience, you only see the face of your instructor, you may be misled. You may have one instructor who has a wry sense of humor, a satirical touch in the give and take of the classroom, and a friendly smile for all students. Then you may have another instructor who appears stern and unapproachable. Are you expected to write differently for each?

The answer lies not so much in the personalities of your instructors but in their shared expectations and assumptions. The audience for legal writing expects rational, logical discussion. Your audience wants to see a clear demonstration of the depth of your understanding, the quality of your analysis, and the clarity of your expression. Your professors don't want unexamined premises; they don't want unanswered questions; they don't want conclusions that are not fully supported. Keeping in mind these expectations in your audience will help you shape your answer, memo, or brief.

Voice. A third consideration as you prepare to write is the voice you will use in your writing. Voice has to do with style, word choice, tone, level of usage, and something called "persona." The persona is the person you project through your writing. It is not you, but it represents you. Just as you may use one voice or style when you talk casually with a friend, and another, more formal, voice when you interview for a job, you may also use many voices in your writing. But voice or persona is more than a level of usage, somewhere between slang and formal; it is more than an awareness of audience. It is a projection of yourself as you would like the reader to see you.

Some law students believe the most impressive persona is one who uses long words and lots of Latin. That assumption doesn't happen to be true. It isn't possible to prescribe an ideal persona or an ideal voice for all students. Each of you already has a voice that is heard in your writing. It is, however, possible to describe a persona that will help you in your writing. Your persona should have a reasonable, thoughtful, logical, analytical voice. Try to explain everything in a straightforward, direct manner. Your voice should be plain and clear.

Analysis.   When you are given a legal writing assignment, you have been given a problem to solve. You must examine the hypothetical situation, distinguish relevant from irrelevant fact, spot the issues, apply the law to the given facts, and lead the reader through your reasoning process to a logical conclusion. You may use a number of problem-solving strategies to analyze the question and identify the issue and the key facts. Later in this textbook we will go into much more detail about spotting issues and applying the law to the facts as we look at specific problems, but for now the following are some helpful analytical techniques to draw on during the pre-writing/planning stage.

Brainstorming.   One technique in analysis is brainstorming. Brainstorming involves an unrestrained flow of ideas. The key to brainstorming is turning off your internal censor that says "No, that can't be right," or "But I'm not sure about that." As you read through the fact pattern, make notes to yourself indicating all possible issues or subissues you can imagine. Note the arguments, reasons, points to consider, supporting evidence—everything you can think of that could bear on the issue. Establishing the relative order and importance of your ideas will come later. Even if you decide to delete later, this free flow of ideas can help you examine all the possibilities you can imagine.

Graphics.   Many of us can understand things better if we prepare a graphic representation of the situation. We can create a time line to help us keep a sequence of events clear in our minds. We can sketch out the details of a traffic accident or the location of houses or property. We can divide assets and liabilities graphically and see their relationships. We can draw lines between related items, circle others, and help ourselves to see things that words may not make clear. Don't be afraid of spending a few minutes with a diagram as part of your analysis.

Anticipating Counterarguments.   Another important technique in analyzing the problem is consciously to anticipate all defenses, counterarguments, and alternative reasoning. You have to examine all issues from all sides before reaching a conclusion. If you don't try to anticipate counterarguments, you may wind up with a one-sided and unconvincing analysis.

This method of analysis is called in rhetoric the proleptical argument. The writer anticipates and counters any opposing argument. Your task is similar. You must identify all defenses and arguments counter to your own position. You must then discuss them, showing how you reached your conclusion. Make this a conscious step so you don't overlook contrary evidence.

Organization.   Some orderly sense must be made of all those notes and diagrams you have compiled. You need to decide what is at issue, what facts are important, and how to demonstrate your impeccable logic as you explain the whole situation to your reader.

Outline.   Too many students, after spending some time determining the issues, skip the next step. They begin drafting before composing any kind of outline. However simple it may be, an outline can help. Taking just a few minutes, even at the beginning of a timed examination, will allow you to spend less time juggling and twisting ideas and evidence while writing. It can prevent those paragraphs that begin, "As should have been mentioned earlier . . ." or, "Similar to the point made in the second paragraph. . . ."

An outline can also prevent those hastily written paragraphs in the margin, connected to the main body of the paper by strange lines and arrows. It can also force you to include all important steps in your reasoning as you examine the outline. Above all, an outline can help you avoid straying from the point.

Writing/Drafting

We have to think about the writing or drafting stage of the writing process in two ways. In the case of a timed law examination, your first draft is also your final draft. You will have time to do some editing and maybe some minor revision. Researched assignments, on the other hand, allow for major revising and editing.

The major difference in writing the two kinds of assignments is that on a first draft you intend to revise, you may feel free to write and develop and may not be conscious of elements you may want to revise or rearrange later. In a timed examination, you have to be more certain of what you want to say before you begin.

As you write either kind of draft, however, you will have a number of writing concerns to keep in mind. You need some ideas about introductions and conclusions; about unity, clarity, and development; and about mechanics, transitions, usage, and style.

Introductions and Conclusions.   It is easy to spend too much time trying to create the right opening line or paragraph in any kind of writing. For students taking a timed examination, too much concern with an introduction is a waste of time. You aren't scoring any points until you say "The first issue is. . . ." Some instructors prefer no introduction at all. For others, a few lines referring to the case or situation in question is enough.

A shoving incident in a ticket line may lead to an action in battery.

An incident that began with a minor traffic citation escalated so that a number of charges may be filed against the driver.

The introduction should only serve to get you into the problem. Once there, you will be able to address the first cause of action, or substantive or procedural issue.

Conclusions should be thought of in two ways. First, each issue you discuss requires that you reach a conclusion. You have to decide if the defendant had a legal privilege to act as he or she did, or if an act was the proximate cause of a particular injury. In that sense, you will have a conclusion for each issue, and each conclusion acts as a signpost showing where you are in your analysis. You will then be able to decide whether someone has liability, or whether someone should be charged with a crime.

You need not have a separate conclusion at the end of a law examination. Because you have already offered conclusions for each issue, a separate paragraph summing up the various actions would only be redundant. The more issues you discuss in your answer, the less effective is a separate concluding paragraph. Instead, be sure that you provide clear, supported conclusions within your paper as you lead the reader through your reasoning on each issue. Separate conclusions become much more important in other kinds of legal writing. The brief and legal memorandum each lead up to a summary conclusion.

Clarity/Style.   The most important goal in legal writing is clarity. You must express your ideas in straightforward, direct language. Write in plain English. Much more detail is provided later in this book on style, but the essence of that chapter is that your writing task is not to impress or to write in legalese, but to explain your reasoning. Your best chance of being impressive is to allow the reader to see the crystal clear quality of your analysis.

Unity/Coherence.   For there to be unity and coherence in a discussion, the relationship among all the parts of the argument must be evident. One idea must lead to the next. You are taking the reader step-by-step through your reasoning process, so the path must be clearly marked. You can't have extraneous comments or lines of reasoning that lead nowhere. To help insure unity and coherence in your writing, two techniques are helpful.

Signposts.   One easy way to let the reader know just where you are and where you are going is through using signposts—words or phrases that call the reader's attention to your point. Some signposts are very mechanical, but still effective.

Three reasons for reaching this conclusion are . . .

The first reason . . .

The second reason . . .

or

Three important issues are present in this case . . .

The first issue . . .

The next issue . . .

Another kind of signpost indicates important points along the way.

The major issue then is . . .

The key issue is whether . . .

Finally, the use of clear and explicit headings will identify the various sections of your answer, memo, or brief. Instead of just going into a discussion of the issue, give the reader a signpost that says you are taking the next step and tells the reader how important that step is.

Transition.   Another helpful way of maintaining unity and guiding your reader through the analysis is with smooth transition. Sometimes transition can be accomplished simply through reference to a previous idea or point. A more mechanical transition is accomplished through the use of words like "also," "however," and "therefore." These transition words should not automatically be plugged in between sentences and paragraphs, but the following list may give you an idea of transition words and their uses.

1. *to indicate an additional idea:* and, also, again, moreover, in addition, next, too, finally, besides, likewise, similarly, another reason.
2. *To indicate an alternative idea:* on the other hand, but, still, however, though, although, yet, nevertheless, of course.
3. *To indicate a conclusion:* therefore, thus, hence, in brief, in short, consequently.
4. *To indicate an example:* for example, for instance, that is, in other words, namely.
5. *To indicate a time relationship:* later, earlier, before, after, when, at the same time.

You can and should think of other techniques demonstrating smooth transition. Remember that it is important to think consciously about the relationships among your points and ideas, and to show those relationships through some kind of transition.

The Mechanics of Writing. While writing effectively is your primary goal, writing correctly is part of the task. Errors in the mechanics of writing lead to several problems. One problem is that no matter how reasonable your arguments are, when you have misspellings or sentence fragments, when your subject and verb don't agree, and when you have used "infer" when you mean "imply," the reader sees the errors and is distracted from your reasoned discussion. Your paper looks worse than it really is. Certain errors (e.g., spelling) lower your "persona" in the estimation of the reader. Writing errors simply call attention to themselves and become red flags even to readers who are not looking for errors.

A second problem is that errors often cannot be separated from the content of your work. The errors themselves may obscure your point or make an assertion ambiguous. When modifiers are misplaced, a reader might not see the proper construction.

Writing error-free prose is not necessarily a guarantee of a good grade or a successful persuasive paper, but the point is that even a well-reasoned and logical writing effort is diminished by careless errors in grammar, punctuation, usage, or spelling. As you write your draft, pay attention to the mechanics as you go along, even though you intend to revise and edit later. Attention to mechanics is especially critical in timed writing assignments because you may not have time to revise or edit after you have completed your answer.

Revising

The next step in the writing process, and one of the most important, is to revise your draft copy. To revise, you must examine your draft, looking at it again from several perspectives; asking questions of yourself; and changing, rearranging, or rewriting various parts.

For most of your writing assignments, certainly all of those written outside of class, revision is a crucial step in the process. Revision is your opportunity to delete sections you don't like, rewrite to clarify, change the order to better emphasize a point, and go into more detail in a section you glossed over initially.

Here are some questions you may ask yourself as you revise.

Is the issue clearly identified?
Have I included the theory of law?

Are there any facts that should be emphasized?
Have I left out any material facts?
Have I reached a logical conclusion?
Is my conclusion completely supported?
Have I shown the reader the steps in my reasoning?
Is my explanation readily understood?
Is my writing clear and direct?

Don't be reluctant to make changes in what you have written. Very few writers produce final copy in their first draft. Most of us have to rearrange, add, delete, and polish before we are satisfied that we have a final draft.

Editing

The last step in the writing process is careful editing. Editing, as we use the term, is a matter of cleaning up the writing by looking for errors, usually in spelling, punctuation, or grammar, and correcting them. The best time to edit an assignment you are doing out of class is only after you have revised and reached a final draft. To edit a first draft is sometimes to substitute the editing phase for the revision phase.

For an in-class, timed writing assignment, you don't have a chance to do much revision. In that situation, our best advice is to emphasize the pre-writing stage and plan carefully because you know you will be turning in your first draft. You can still have time to edit, so you should try to save a few minutes to reread your paper looking for errors. If you can eliminate any careless errors in your answer, you can at least prevent the reader from being distracted or influenced by them.

CONCLUSION

In your legal studies, you will be asked to write various kinds of legal documents and analyses of legal issues. You will write answers to law examination questions, legal memoranda, and legal briefs. As you write your law school assignments and as you write in practice, you must remember that writing is a process involving a number of steps and stages. You must engage in the pre-writing stage of brainstorming, analyzing, organizing, and outlining. You must draft your document, writing as clearly and directly as possible while remembering to provide logical signposts and all supporting arguments. And you must not fail to revise carefully, considering the questions for revision we have provided in this chapter. Finally, you must proofread and edit before you can submit your work with confidence.

As you proceed through this textbook, you will see how we have applied the writing process in detail to the legal writing you will be expected to do. If you remember that writing is a process and not a simple burst of inspired sentences, you can work through all the stages in the process to produce clear, well-developed briefs, memos, and answers on law exams.

CHAPTER TWO
The Strategy
of Legal Persuasion

INTRODUCTION

As stated in Chapter 1, there is a definite, identifiable strategy that is most likely to be successful in legal persuasion. At this point we should distinguish this strategy from specific techniques for writing on law problems. *Strategy* involves the overall plan that writers have when they set out to persuade a reader of the correctness of their legal points. Writers know, in general, that they must be logical, concise, and clear. They know that they must avoid logical and emotional fallacies. They also know that their audience expects them to "sound like lawyers," not in the sense of loading their papers with legal jargon, but in the sense of tight organization and direct language. On the other hand, the *techniques* for writing answers to law examination questions are specific devices that writers can use to tear apart a question, organize an answer, and cover all of the vital issues within a brief time. In this chapter strategies will be discussed. In later chapters we will present techniques.

ANSWERING THE LAW EXAMINATION QUESTION

One of the most frustrating experiences for law students is learning that what they thought was a brilliant answer to an exam question got a mediocre grade. One of the most frustrating things for a law professor is trying to tell a student why a particular paper got the mediocre grade. It's easy to show a writer that he or she has missed some of the major issues in a problem, but when the student has mentioned all of the important issues there is bound to be some misunderstanding. It is not that law professors don't know what they want—indeed, there is a good deal of agreement among them as to whether a particular paper is good or poor. Rather, there is great difficulty in expressing to a student why it is that a particular paper is not written the way a professor wants it written, why it doesn't sound "lawyerlike." To develop a strategy for legal persuasion, then, we must examine what it means to "sound like a lawyer."

On the front of a bar examination is a set of instructions indicating, in general, the kind of answer that will be successful on the exam. In a very important sense, these instructions outline a strategy of legal persuasion. They tell the candidate what it means to sound like a lawyer. Consequently, as a point of departure for our attempt to define the elements of the strategy of legal persuasion, we can use the instructions by bar examiners on a bar examination.

We have taken the instructions from the California Bar Examination as an example, because they are comprehensive, concise, and representative of principles that can apply to all legal persuasion. We will begin by quoting the instructions in their entirety and then attempt to examine carefully each point the bar examiners make. The result of that analysis will be a strategy useful for law school examinations.

The following instructions appear as a preface to the essay examination questions:

> An answer should demonstrate your ability to analyze the facts presented by the question, to select the material from the immaterial facts, and to discern the points upon which the case turns. It should show your knowledge and understanding of the pertinent principles and theories of law, their relationships to each other, and their qualifica-

tions and limitations. It should evidence your ability to apply the law to the facts given, and to reason logically in a lawyerlike manner to a sound conclusion from the premises adopted. Try to demonstrate your proficiency in using and applying legal principles rather than a mere memory of them.

An answer containing only a statement of your conclusions will receive little credit. State fully the reasons that support them. All points should be thoroughly discussed. Although your answer should be complete, you should not volunteer information or discuss legal doctrines that are not necessary or pertinent to the solution of the problem.

Let us now consider each of the elements of these instructions separately.

LEGAL ANALYSIS

The first part of the instructions focuses on the need for careful analysis of the question:

An answer should demonstrate your ability to analyze the facts presented by the question, to select the material from the immaterial facts, and to discern the points upon which the case turns.

The three important elements in this instruction—analysis, selection, and discernment—have to be examined carefully.

Analysis

This process is what goes on in the mind of the lawyer or student when confronted with the facts of a particular problem. Because analysis is the ability that most of law school is directed toward developing, we can't provide any simple rules or directions. We can, however, make several observations. First, one of the important goals of the strategy of legal persuasion is to demonstrate, in writing, the analysis that has gone on in the writer's mind. Second, because this process depends upon "knowing the law," you need to have learned the law in a given area in order to analyze effectively.

For instance, you might be told that "Gene wrote a letter to the local newspaper in which he said that Congressman Smith watched pornographic movies in his basement while beating himself with licorice whips." An analysis by the average reader might only involve asking whether this allegation about Congressman Smith was true or false. However, a law student's analysis would probably include an examination of the elements of libel, invasion of privacy, intentional infliction of emotional distress, and privileged statements.

This doesn't mean that you will just have to wait until you've learned all of the law to start learning to write like a lawyer. It does mean, however, that to analyze facts, you will have to have some rules in mind to apply. In the following chapters we use law questions that present facts and simplified rules of law. They are similar to questions encountered in law school. You will be asked to apply the rules to the facts, then follow the strategies and techniques we discuss as you write your answer. Still, that first step, analysis, is a matter of viewing the facts with the law in mind.

Selection

Selection of material facts is one important step in the process of analysis. To select important from unimportant facts, you must have a principle of selection. In law, that principle is generally provided by the elements of a particular law. For instance, if assault were defined as an "intentional, unprivileged, unconsented act that causes reasonable apprehension of an imminent touching," you would have a principle for selecting the material facts in a hypothetical situation. That is, you would know that assault requires (a) an act or gesture of some sort, (b) that the gesture be intentional (as opposed to involuntary), (c) that the gesture cause apprehension in another, (d) that the apprehension be reasonable, and (e) that the apprehension be of an imminent touching. Furthermore, you would know that if the actor is privileged to make that gesture, or if the person against whom the gesture is directed has consented to that action, there can be no assault. Consider the following problem.

It was noon on the day of a predicted solar eclipse. Brian parked illegally, spit on the sidewalk in violation of a city ordinance, and made an obscene telephone call. Several hours later he was approached by Fred, a minister who had spent most of his life providing food and clothing for victims of natural disasters. Fred, who was a foot taller than Brian, said, "I see that you are possessed by an evil demon and I must beat it out of you." Brian replied, "Don't you touch me!" Fred swung at him and missed. Brian ducked. Brian sued for assault. What result?

It is easy to see that the predicted solar eclipse is an immaterial fact in determining whether an assault occurred. Law students would also easily recognize that the facts about the prior actions and character of both parties would be irrelevant. Facts become relevant according to the way they relate to the theory of law involved. It is clear that a knowledge of the elements of assault is necessary to provide a principle for selecting the important from the unimportant facts. Therefore, once you are given rules of law to apply to the factual situation, you can decide which facts are going to be important in your discussion.

Discernment

Discernment is a matter of deciding which points in the analysis are truly crucial and therefore worthy of considerable discussion, and which points are necessary, but either obvious or minor, and therefore worthy only of brief discussion. When your time is limited, it is impossible to spend equal amounts of time successfully on every point. If you discuss every point as if it were a major legal issue, you will not have demonstrated your ability to distinguish among major and minor issues. If you discuss every point as if it were a minor issue, you will have an incomplete discussion. In either case you would not have demonstrated that you could discern the major points. Consider the following example.

Suppose that battery is defined as "the harmful or offensive touching of another that is intentional, unconsented, and unprivileged." You can see that battery requires (a) a touching, (b) that the touching be either harmful or offensive to the person touched, and (c) that the touching be the result of an intentional (as opposed to an involuntary) act. Furthermore, you can see that if the person touched had consented to being touched (as when you agree to play in a football game), or if the person doing the touching is privileged to touch the other person (as is a policeman who is making a legal arrest or a person who is acting in self-defense), then there can be no battery.

Consider the following fact pattern.

> Doug and Bob were standing at a bus stop talking. Doug became angry with Bob and began calling him abusive names and challenging him to fight. When Bob did not respond, Doug took a swing at Bob and missed. As Doug was trying again to punch Bob, Doug was hit by a punch from Bob that broke Doug's jaw. Doug sues for battery. What result?

If you were to spend equal amounts of time discussing whether there was an intentional act by Bob, whether there was a touching, whether it was harmful, and whether it was consented to by Doug, you would show a distinct lack of discernment. While each of the points of law must be mentioned to establish that there was a battery under the definition given, two issues are paramount. First, there is the question of whether Doug consented to the touching by provoking the fight—and is therefore precluded from suing in battery. (There are differences of opinion between jurisdictions as to whether one can consent to a "breach of the peace.") Secondly, did Bob exercise a legitimate privilege of self-defense? As a matter of strategy, you must plan to identify the crucial issues in a fact situation and spend most of your time discussing them. Don't spend so much time displaying what you know about the obvious aspects that you don't have time to discuss the *vital* point on which the case turns.

LEGAL RELATIONSHIPS

In analyzing a question, you must also make some strategic decisions about legal relationships. According to the California Bar Examiners, an answer

> should show your *knowledge and understanding* of the pertinent principles and theories of law, their *relationship* to each other, and their *qualifications and limitations.*

We have already discussed the importance of discerning which are the pertinent theories of law and how this rests on your sound analysis of the hypothetical fact situation. Next, you have to decide how you can show your knowledge and understanding of those legal theories, your grasp of their relationships to one another, and your realization of their qualifications and limitations.

Knowledge and Understanding

For most students it is not difficult to show knowledge of the law. Assuming that you have studied the material, you can usually regurgitate the "rule of law." Having done that, however, you are still far from being home free. Legal questions would hardly be worth posing if they could be solved by a simple application of a "rule." Indeed, if everything were that clear cut, there would be no need for judges or lawyers. We could simply feed the information into a computer and get back a "just" decision.

Both in the "real" world and in the fairy-tale world of law problems, where there are never any simple crimes, contracts, or wrongs, everything has complications. Deciding—or conjecturing— who should prevail in a particular case depends on your ability to understand the foundations and rationale for a particular rule of law. Students learn case law by reading appellate cases. An appellate decision provides a ruling on legal issues raised in the appeal and provides a rationale for the holding. As students study the cases, they learn to see the qualifications and limitations of the law.

Keeping in mind the definition of battery ("a harmful or offensive touching of another that is intentional, unprivileged, and unconsented"), consider the following fact situation.

> Howard was taking a potential buyer of his tennis clothing store to lunch at the Ritz Hotel. The lunch was buffet-style, and they were both standing in the serving line, holding their plates. Suddenly the manager of the hotel came up to Howard and shouted, "We don't serve people in short pants and tennis shoes here! This is a fine establishment." With that he grabbed Howard's plate and pulled it away. Assume that the manager is not privileged in his actions. Does Howard have a cause of action for battery?

It would be easy for you to state the "rule of law" involved (the definition of a battery), but that doesn't help much. It is crucial in resolving this problem to decide whether there was an "offensive touching of another." Many students have difficulty in answering this type of question, not because they can't figure it out, but because they assume that touching the plate either is or is not a touching of the person. Then they simply state that conclusion.

But to give a satisfactory answer to a critical reader—and law professors tend to be careful and critical readers—you must understand the rationale behind the rule. As a Texas court said in a similar case, "Since the essence of the plaintiff's grievance consists in the offense to the dignity involved in the unpermitted and intentional invasion of the inviolability of his person and not in any physical harm done to his body, it is not necessary that the plaintiff's actual body be disturbed."[1] If you understood that this was the essence of the battery action, you would have no difficulty in making an analogy that would cover snatching someone's hat, grabbing a package from someone's hands, or taking someone's pocketbook. In each instance, a simple statement of the rule involved would not suffice. You would need to explain that you had decided that there was a touching of the person because the object that had been grabbed was so closely associated with the person that it could not be taken without offending the dignity of that individual. Even in the law questions we provide (with a rule of law attached), you must discuss *why* you believe it should or should not be applied. You can't just state the rule and jump to a conclusion.

One further word of caution seems important here. Sometimes students mistake history for understanding. They state a rule of law and then mention its historical development. In so doing, they don't demonstrate their understanding of and perspective on the rule (which might be very helpful). Instead, they simply offer a road map, showing where the rule has been and what towns it passed through in getting to its present location. This is not the same as demonstrating an understanding of the rule of law. Its chief merit would be in an essay for a developmental legal history course, and even there it might be inappropriate.

What is important, and this is the chief strategy with which you should be concerned, is spending as little space as possible on a bald statement of the "rule of law." Instead, devote your time, as well as significant space in your answer, to demonstrating that you understand the nature of the rule you are using by applying it to the facts given.

[1] *Fisher v. Carrousel Motor Hotel, Inc.* 424 S.W. 2d 627, 629 (1967).

Types of Relationships

A fact situation usually requires discussion of a number of "rules of law." Because these rules are often related to one another, you must discuss them in the light of that relationship. In other words, as law professors are fond of saying, "the law is a seamless web," with the actions, rights, and liabilities of each of the parties affecting all of the other parties. However, if we simply told you that the law is a seamless web and that you must take account of all the relevant legal relationships in planning an answer, you would be heartily justified in throwing this book in the trash or demanding a refund from the publisher. Consequently, we shall try to examine four types of relationships between legal principles and theories and develop a strategy for dealing with each.

Civil/Criminal. The easiest relationship to see is also the one that provides the simplest strategic problem. The same act may give rise to both civil and criminal liability. That is, when someone holds up a liquor store she may have committed both a crime (robbery) and a civil offense (the tort of conversion). In the first instance, it is the state she will have to answer to in a criminal action. In the second, the owner of the liquor store may be able to sue her to recover the money that was lost. The strategy here is simple. In a law exam question, the subject matter of the course (e.g., torts, criminal law) will direct the focus of your answer. Moreover, if you were involved as an adversary attempting to defend the holdup person, you would be defending her from either civil or criminal liability. Again, you would simply devote your energies to the one aspect of the case with which you were dealing. In a memo you would have to consider each aspect separately.

Wrongs That Often Occur Together. A second relationship may develop because one wrong usually entails another. For instance, while there can be an assault without a battery and vice versa, the two usually occur together. Consequently, the presence of one should always alert you to the possible presence of the other. If one of the wrongs clearly occurred, you should discuss that first and go on to discuss the possibility of the other having occurred. This might be called the strategy of "at least." At least assault occurred and possibly a battery, too. Therefore, you may have as a fallback position the lesser wrong. That is, even if you do not succeed in showing that the gravest offense occurred, you will have made a clear case for the lesser offense.

Legally Dependent Wrongs. A third type of relationship is very similar to the second. In some instances, whether a particular wrong has occurred depends on whether another independent wrong occurred or was contemplated. For instance, for one to be an accomplice to a crime, the crime itself must have been committed. Consider the following fact situation.

> Stan was a member of the Middletown police department working as an undercover policeman. He was contacted by Ollie, who suggested that they hold up the neighborhood liquor store. The men entered the liquor store together. Stan pointed a gun at the owner of the store and handed him a note that read: "I am a police officer. Hand me your money and pretend this is a robbery. I will return the money later." The owner did as he had been instructed, and the two men left. Half an hour later Stan came back and returned the money. Was Ollie guilty of being an accomplice to a robbery?

If we were to assume that one of the necessary elements of robbery is the intent to deprive someone permanently of his or her property, both the solution and a strategy suggest themselves. Because we know that the target crime (robbery) must have been committed for there to be an accomplice liability, we would first examine whether that crime had been committed. But even if we conclude that the target crime had not been committed, we cannot ignore the question of accomplice liability. Because questions are often drafted so that the answer to the first issue is not clear cut, you will often have to consider the second issue conditionally. "If there were a robbery, accomplice liability is still in question." If we decided that the target crime had been committed, or if there was any possibility that it had been committed, we would still discuss the elements of accomplice liability and reach a conclusion. Whenever you decide that the existence of a certain legal fact will determine the rest of your analysis, discuss that fact first.

Multiple Wrongs/Single Act. The fourth type of relationship we can identify involves a single act that may potentially offend a number of different civil interests. For instance, if Gene were to tell Bill (in the presence of Congressman Smith) that Congressman Smith watched pornographic movies in his basement while beating himself with licorice whips, the congressman might have a number of potential actions against Gene. He might be able to sue for defamation, invasion of privacy, or intentional infliction of emotional distress. Suppose further that if the allegation is true, there can be no defamation, but that truth is no defense to either of the other actions.

Confronted by this multitude of potential actions, your strategy should be to attempt to eliminate some as soon as possible in order to devote most of your time to the others. To do this you should first inquire whether there is a single element that distinguishes one of the possible actions from all of the others. In this example we know that if the allegation is true, there can be no defamation. Thus, we should first determine whether the allegation is true. If so, we can eliminate the possibility of defamation and spend more time discussing the other potential torts. If we cannot determine that the allegation is true from the facts given, as in this hypothetical situation, we must adopt a different tactic.

Where there are many potential torts and no single factor present that would allow you to eliminate one immediately, you must look for those elements common to all of the torts. After you have found them, you should discuss them first and only once. Avoid repetition. Then you can move on to those further elements of the different torts that arise from a specific fact situation.

QUALIFICATIONS AND LIMITATIONS

The major problem students seem to encounter when discussing the qualifications and limitations of various actions is failing to recognize that there is something that is being qualified or limited, and that it must be discussed. Put another way, you must at least mention the prima facie case (those elements of the wrong that must be present for there to be legal liability) before you can discuss the defenses (the limitations and qualifications of the legal theory). For example, as we have discussed previously, a person may be privileged to touch another and consequently not liable for battery. Consider the following facts.

Melvin was a student at the East Newark Free School. One day, to express his latent creativity, he began to spray-paint the principal's Volkswagen in a tony shade of mauve. Melvin's teacher saw what he was doing and grabbed the can of paint from his hand. She then acted out her anger by smacking Melvin smartly across his bottom. Melvin—through his parents—sues the teacher for battery. What result?

While you might simply say there is no liability because teachers have a privilege to administer reasonable discipline to their pupils, that sort of answer would not demonstrate your awareness that "privilege" is a limitation of battery. Rather, your strategy should be to establish quickly that there was the *possibility* of battery and then go on to examine the question of privilege. In this fact situation, it might be worth exploring the question of whether this was "reasonable discipline" or just blind rage on the part of the teacher. In any case, you would have shown your understanding of battery as well as its qualifications and limitations.

USING THE FACTS

After stressing the importance of analyzing the question and demonstrating your understanding of legal relationships, the California Bar Examiners give the following additional advice about what an answer should do.

It should evidence your ability to *apply the law to the facts* given, and to *reason logically* in a lawyerlike manner to a *sound conclusion from the premises adopted.*

Once again, this advice breaks down into recommendations in three areas: using the facts, reasoning logically, and adopting premises.

Errors in Using the Facts

It seems so obvious that you must apply the law to the facts you have been given that you might wonder why the bar examiners bother mentioning it. Indeed, you can probably apply the rules of law to the facts almost automatically and come up with an "answer," a solution to the problem of who is liable or who is guilty. However, for many people this is an almost subconscious process, and its end result is an "answer" that they then blithely write as their answer to the question posed. What they fail to do is to reproduce the mental process that went into their determination of an answer. This is a fatal mistake. Your answer must show *how*—not simply *that*—you used the facts in your analysis. Let's look at three common problems you might encounter in your attempts to use the facts, and then check examples of these errors and discover a strategy for demonstrating your ability to use the facts.

Failure to Use the Facts.   The most common error students make is that they fail to use the facts at all. They read the facts, determine what the potential legal actions are, and then write a discussion of the law. This discussion is followed by a conclusion about the liabilities of the parties involved. Sometimes the student notices that the answer is awfully short and puts in some fillers to lengthen it. These addenda may be a discussion of the history of a particular law, or some speculation about what would have been the liabilities of the parties under an entirely different set of facts, or simply a paraphrase of what the student has already concluded.

For instance, having concluded that Melvin's teacher had a privilege to strike him, one student went on to say:

> This privilege comes from a theory that teachers often take the place of parents in the schoolroom situation. Thus since parents can discipline their children, teachers can too. The teacher's privilege is even more clear where the student is disrupting a class or injuring other children. There, as here, the teacher has a privilege to strike the child, even without the parent's consent.

What this student failed to do was to even consider whether there was any battery that Melvin could allege and whether the "teacher's privilege" would apply in this particular situation. Instead, we have a general discussion of privilege and some speculation about a set of facts that has not been given in this problem. Such fillers don't help. Indeed, they may even convince the reader that the student doesn't know how to select material facts and has no understanding of the pertinent principles of law.

Restatement of the Facts. Another common error—especially among students who have once been told that they must use the facts—is the restatement of the facts in the answer. This type of answer usually begins by looking like a *Reader's Digest* condensation of the hypothetical facts, often with the articles omitted. There is a major difference between using the facts and simply repeating them. In the former instance, the student shows an ability to connect facts of legal significance with theories of law; in the latter, the student shows only an ability to condense.

The reason that students often fall into this trap is that this type of answer actually contains all of the correct elements. The condensation of the facts is usually followed by a statement of the applicable law, and then a series of legal conclusions. However, all of the logical connections remain in the student's mind and must be guessed at by the reader. The student relies on the reader to connect a fact or series of facts in the first paragraph with a legal theory in the third paragraph to arrive at a conclusion that is stated in the sixth paragraph. It is as if you had contracted to have a house built and the builder had presented you with the lumber, a blueprint, and a picture of a finished house. Everything you need for the house is there, but the work has been left up to you.

Juxtaposition of the Facts. The most sophisticated kind of failure to show an ability to use the facts occurs when students present facts, legal theories, and conclusions all mixed together, often in a single paragraph. The facts are usually appropriate to the legal theory presented, and the conclusion is usually an acceptable one. However, while the reader no longer has to glance from paragraph to paragraph to find the elements of a good answer, the specific way in which a particular fact is connected to a legal theory is still only in the student's mind. The reader is forced to articulate the connection for himself or herself. Students who do this are like builders who put all of the pieces in the right place but fail to nail them together.

It is essential that you *write out every single mental step* that went into your determination of how the legal principles are related to the facts you were given. As a matter of technique you should continually ask yourself "Why?" Why does this fact show that a particular element of a legal theory is present? If the "because" is not clearly stated in your answer, you must add another sentence showing how you got from a particular fact to known legal theory. Don't make the reader leap from point to point. Take small steps. It might be worthwhile to view your job not as answering a particular question, but as *explaining* to a client how you reached a certain conclusion. Picture yourself with a client who will not make a single move without understanding all of the reasons. Only when you have explained every detail of your reasoning can you be sure that you have demonstrated your ability to relate legal principles to the facts given.

One final word of caution. Law students often fear that they will insult a professor's intelligence by failing to leap magnificently from peak to peak in their argument, without glancing fearfully at the chasm below. "Good grief," they say, "the professor knows that. There's no reason to explain that simple point." Of course the professor is well aware of all the legal theories and how they relate to the facts he or she has given you. After all, he or she wrote the question. That's not the point. For purposes of examining students, professors adopt the pose of cantankerous old Uncle Melvin from Missouri who always says, "Show me. And don't go giving me none of your fancy five-dollar words." Show your professor. Step-by-step.

REASONING LOGICALLY

Logical reasoning is so important to legal writing that we have devoted all of Chapter 6 to it. However, we can take a brief look here at what it is that we often identify as "reasoning in a lawyerlike manner."

In examining a problem, an ideal lawyer would show an awareness of language, a tendency to look carefully at all of the facts before reaching a conclusion, and a habit of considering both sides of an argument. When lay persons look at a simple statement, they are too often likely to assume immediately that they understand what it means. A lawyer, however, is likely to examine each word in the statement and find alternative, less obvious meanings. Now this can be a damned annoying habit, particularly when there is a great deal of apparent agreement and this consideration produces some dissent. But lawyers are trained to look for less obvious meanings because they know that words do not have a single meaning and that many disagreements occur because people who are using the same word do not mean the same thing.

So, too, with our ideal lawyer's tendency to look carefully at all the facts before reaching any conclusion. We all depend on facts to reach conclusions, but we often jump to conclusions without carefully considering all the facts, or we fail to consider what we know in the light of our own preconceptions and assumptions.

Riddles work on this principle. For instance, "Ronald has two coins in his hand that total fifty-five cents. One of them is not a half-dollar. What are the two coins?" Were you to jump to the conclusion that a half-dollar cannot be in Ronald's hand, you would never solve the riddle. But if you carefully consider the statement "one of them is not a half-dollar," you will realize that it allows the possibility that *the other* is a half-dollar. That makes the problem simple. Take another example.

> Barry was the son of a very protective doctor who threatened to sue any other doctor who treated Barry. While his father was out of town, Barry was in an accident and was treated for a sprained wrist. No suit was brought. Why?

Unless you are willing to examine the facts in the light of preconceptions you may hold, the problem is a difficult one. However, if you consider the obvious fact that not all doctors are men, the problem is easy to solve. Barry's mother was the "very protective doctor," and it was she who treated him. Or, perhaps Barry, too, was out of town. Again, one of the distinguishing marks of lawyerlike reasoning is examining all of the facts with great care before arriving at a conclusion.

Finally, and perhaps most importantly for students, lawyers are trained to look at both sides of a problem. While almost invariably they will be in the position of arguing only one side of a case, they know that they must consider what arguments will be used against them. An old adage holds that, "One who knows only one's own side of an argument knows little of that." (We have more to say about this in the chapter on logic, but you may remember the term "proleptical argument" from Chapter 1.) Always bearing in mind that an adversary will present the best case that can be made for the other side, lawyers examine a set of facts with an eye to both the strengths and weaknesses of their position. Thus, one of the hallmarks of a lawyerlike analysis is that it does not fail to consider a fact simply because that fact would be adverse to the position that must be argued. Rather, the analysis takes even the adverse facts into account and builds an argument with them in mind.

When it comes to presenting an argument, our ideal lawyer would pay great attention to organizing the points and presenting them in an orderly fashion. That lawyer might say: "There are three major issues here." Or, "We needn't even consider whether X occurred unless we can establish that there was a Y." Both of these statements are signs that the raw data have been organized into an argument. The argument is then presented in an orderly fashion. No matter what distractions are presented, lawyers attempt to stick to the point they are discussing before handling counterarguments or moving on to the next point. In this way, they can be sure that the argument is at least understood, if not accepted.

If you are attempting to show that you can reason in a lawyerlike manner, all of these observations should suggest a strategy. You must examine all of the facts carefully, consider both sides, organize your argument, and present it in an orderly fashion. Perhaps at the moment all of this sounds like nothing more than advice to be virtuous, but if you master the techniques of legal writing in the following chapters and the elements of legal logic in Chapter 6, you can be assured that you will wind up reasoning in a lawyerlike manner.

ADOPTING PREMISES

While the way in which you reason will be the subject of the chapter on logic and argument, it is important to pay some attention to the way in which you go about adopting premises. Usually, you will not have every item of information you need to make a logical argument with the facts you are given. Consequently, you will have to make some inferences from the facts in order to arrive at the premises you will be using to justify your position on the issue. There are two vital strategies for you to remember. First, you must use high-probability inferences in adopting premises. Second, you must state explicitly what your premises are.

High-Probability Inferences

The first strategy sounds far more complex than it is. Suppose that you are playing pool and that you hit the cue ball so that it strikes the eight ball. A number of possibilities exist. The eight ball may go into a pocket, into a cushion, or off the table entirely. It is also possible that the eight ball is defective and will crack when the cue ball hits it. It is also possible (although only remotely so) that your worst enemy has cleverly replaced the eight ball with a bomb that looks like an eight ball, so that when the cue ball hits it there will be an explosion that takes your life. Absurd? Perhaps so, but some statistician could probably figure out the odds for the eight-ball explosion.

Notice the differences among the possibilities we have mentioned. In the first instance, all of the facts are as we normally find them. That is, our experience tells us that when the cue ball hits the eight ball, the latter is propelled in some direction. (Exactly how far it goes, and where, probably depends on how much of your time you spend in pool halls.) In the second instance, the occurrence of the event depends on the assumption that one of the elements is other than as it appears. That is, it depends on the eight ball's having a hidden defect. Finally, in the last instance, the occurrence of the possible outcome depends on the assumption of at least two (probably more) circumstances that are not apparent. You must have an enemy who wants to kill you, and the enemy must have cleverly replaced the eight ball with a bomb.

Let us move back a step and examine the three possible outcomes more abstractly. In the first instance you must make no additional assumptions in order to infer what the outcome of hitting the eight ball will be. In the second instance you must make one additional assumption; in the third, two. If you apply your own experience to the facts, you are likely to say that the first or second outcome is the most likely and the last the least likely to occur. As a general rule, then, we can say that the more assumptions you have to adopt to make your inference, the less probable that inference is. Put another way, the first inference is a high-probability inference and the third is a low-probability inference.

Now let's try to apply this to a legal problem. Let us suppose, for the sake of an example, that the following rules are applied to determine whether someone is liable to another for false imprisonment. "1. A person is liable to another for false imprisonment if (a) he or she acts intending to confine the other person within fixed boundaries, (b) his or her act results in confinement of the other person, and (c) the other person is aware of being confined. (d) If a person forces another to choose between forfeiting something of value and remaining within fixed boundaries, this shows an intention to confine the other." Now consider the following facts.

Ms. Smith went to the Elegant Cow restaurant and ordered an extra-rare steak. The waiter brought her one that was burned to a crisp. She refused to accept the steak, and when the waiter told her that he would not bring her another, she got up to leave. As she was walking out, the manager of the restaurant grabbed her custom-designed pocketbook and told her that she could not have it back unless she paid for the steak. He refused to return the pocketbook, and Ms. Smith remained for one hour while he insisted that she pay for the food she had sent back. Finally, he gave her back the pocketbook and she left. Is the manager liable for false imprisonment? You may assume that Ms. Smith was not legally obligated to pay for the burned steak.

One of the premises you would have to use in arguing that the manager would be liable for false imprisonment is that he acted "intending to confine" Ms. Smith. The facts do not explicitly state that he acted with that intent. However, you may be able to infer that intent from the facts you do have and the applicable rule.

The easiest and most likely inference you could make is that because the pocketbook was "custom-designed," it was "something of value" and that according to the rule, this shows that the manager intended to confine Ms. Smith. This inference requires no additional assumptions about the contents of the pocketbook. While an assumption that there was a lot of money in the pocketbook may not be terribly unlikely, it would be a lower-probability assumption.

Finally, you might argue that the pocketbook contained the only copy of the Smith family's secret recipe for their famous cough drops and that, therefore, it was "something of value" within the meaning of the rule. This last inference requires at least two assumptions. First, that Ms. Smith is of the family that makes famous cough drops from a secret recipe, and second, that Ms. Smith happened to be carrying the recipe with her. While this may display a certain amount of creativity on your part, this inference is of a much lower probability than either of the others. Consequently, the premise that you would adopt from this inference (i.e., that the manager had the requisite intent) in arguing that false imprisonment occurred would be less well supported than in either of the first two examples.

Usually students make this third kind of inference only when (a) they are desperate because they cannot find any way of connecting the facts with a rule, or (b) they have written too summary an answer to a question and know, by the amount of time they have left, that they must have missed something. Whichever is the case, you must recognize low-probability inferences and avoid adopting premises based on them.

Stating the Premises Explicitly

Having examined why you must use high-probability inferences in arriving at the premises you use in your argument, we must look at the second part of your strategy: stating your premises explicitly. Unfortunately, things are likely to get a bit confusing here. The problem is that the word "premise" means (according to the dictionary) "a proposition antecedently supposed or proved as a basis of an argument or inference." If we look at the definition of false imprisonment that we have been using, we will see that each of the first three statements (a, b, and c) is a premise in the argument that the manager is liable to Ms. Smith for false imprisonment. That is, if we can show that he acted intending to confine Ms. Smith within the boundaries of the restaurant, that his actions resulted in her confinement, and that she was aware that she was confined, we will be able to logically infer that the manager is liable to Ms. Smith for false imprisonment. Obviously, part of your strategy is to state each of these premises explicitly. However, an answer is really a chain of connected arguments.

Let us examine how we reached the premise that the manager acted intending to confine Ms. Smith within the boundaries of the restaurant. According to the rules we were given, forcing someone to "choose between forfeiting something of value and remaining within fixed boundaries . . . shows an intention to confine the other." Thus, according to this rule, if we can show that the manager forced Ms. Smith to make such a choice, we are entitled to conclude that he intended to confine her. Let us look at the relevant facts. We are told that the manager took Ms. Smith's "custom-designed pocketbook," that he "told her that she could not have it back unless she paid for the steak," and that "Ms. Smith remained for one hour." According to the facts, then, Ms. Smith had three choices open to her when the manager took the pocketbook:

1. She could pay for the steak she had refused and leave with her pocketbook.
2. She could leave without paying and forfeit her pocketbook.
3. She could remain in the restaurant.

Because one of the choices is clearly "remaining within fixed boundaries," we must ask if the other two choices both involve "forfeiting [giving up] something of value." If you decide that both the money to pay for the steak and the pocketbook qualify as "something of value," you must state that premise explicitly. An error students commonly make is *not* stating explicitly the premises they have adopted.

Of course, this all probably looks like plain common sense. Indeed, for the sake of emphasis, we have chosen an easy example. The hidden premise in this argument (that the pocketbook is something of value) is a small one, and you could probably get away with not mentioning it. But many students have been chagrined to find that what seems to them too obvious to mention is not obvious to the person reading their exams, or that even if it is obvious, the reader sometimes wants to see *how* a conclusion was reached and *what* premises were adopted, rather than just a conclusion. (We will be discussing writing only conclusions shortly.)

There are, then, two vital strategies to be remembered when adopting premises: first, you must use high-probability inferences; second, you must explicitly state your premises.

USING AND APPLYING LEGAL PRINCIPLES

In what is essentially a summary of the strategies we have been discussing thus far, the California Bar Examiners advise writers to do the following.

Try to demonstrate your proficiency in using and applying legal principles rather than a mere memory of them.

What is crucial in this advice is the distinction between "mere memory" and "using and applying" principles of law. Not much needs to be said about "mere memory." Clearly, if you simply state a "rule" of law, you have demonstrated "mere memory" of that rule. We do not mean to imply that it is unnecessary to know or remember any rules of law. Obviously, that is the starting point from which you begin your analysis. However, it is far more important to demonstrate your proficiency in using and applying legal rules that you know, and it is the strategy for demonstrating that ability to which we must pay some attention.

A legal theory, or rule, is a tool that the student must use to make an accurate legal analysis. Remember, we said earlier that the rule provides a principle that you must use in separating the material from the immaterial facts in a hypothetical fact situation. It is only in light of the rule that you can know what are important facts that must be taken into account in your analysis. The way you demonstrate your proficiency in the use of this tool is by explaining why you have chosen to consider an issue or why you have chosen to dismiss it.

Let us reconsider an example we looked at earlier. Examine this fact pattern.

> It was noon on the day of a predicted solar eclipse. Brian parked illegally, spit on the sidewalk in violation of a city ordinance, and made an obscene telephone call. Several hours later he was approached by Fred, a minister who had spent most of his life providing food and clothing for victims of natural disasters. Fred, who was a foot taller than Brian, said, "I see that you are possessed by an evil demon and I must beat it out of you." Brian replied, "Don't you touch me!" Fred swung at him and missed. Brian ducked. Brian sued for assault. What result?

If we take as our rule that assault is "an intentional, unprivileged, unconsented act that causes reasonable apprehension of an imminent touching," we can readily identify two different kinds of facts in this example. First, there are two facts of no apparent legal significance: that it was noon, and that there was to be a solar eclipse on that day. (Had we not been told that Brian ducked, it might have been necessary to know the time of day to be sure that he could see the blow aimed at him.) Second, there are facts that appear to have some legal significance. All of Brian's illegal acts, the conversation, and the acts that transpired between Brian and Fred all *appear* to have some legal significance. However, if we examine the facts in the light of the legal principle we are using (assault), it becomes clear that none of the illegal acts that occurred prior to the encounter between Brian and Fred could have any legal significance for our analysis. To demonstrate your ability to use a legal principle rather than just remember it, you need only state a brief reason for dismissing facts of apparent legal significance. Here it might be sufficient to say, "None of Brian's potentially criminal acts could have any bearing on his assault action because they occurred before his encounter with Fred and were unrelated to it."

What you must remember is that it is essential to give a reason for either considering or dismissing a fact of apparent legal significance. This will help you demonstrate your proficiency in using legal principles.

STATEMENTS OF CONCLUSIONS ONLY

According to the California Bar Examiners,

> An answer containing only a statement of your conclusions will receive little credit. State fully the reasons that support them. All points should be thoroughly discussed.

A legal argument that contains only a statement of conclusions receives little credit either in terms of a grade or as a matter of inspiring agreement on the part of a reader. When you offer a totally conclusory argument, you are saying no more than "This is what I think. Believe me." That is not enough for legal arguments.

Many students have difficulty spotting their own conclusory answers because failures to support fully a conclusion come in many different forms. We have already talked about most of them, but perhaps a brief review would help to fix these potential danger areas in your mind. We can examine three different types of conclusory answers: inadequate use of the facts, incomplete reasoning, and failure to make legal principles clear.

Inadequate Use of the Facts

In discussing the ways in which students inadequately use the facts, we mentioned three problems: failure to use the facts, restatement of the facts, and juxtaposition of facts and law. The first problem, inadequate use of the facts, usually occurs because you have gotten so caught up in your legal analysis that you assume that the reader knows the factual basis on which you relied in reaching legal conclusions. While the reader may have a copy of the hypothetical fact situation right there on the desk, it is unlikely that he or she will undertake the task of supplying the appropriate facts for each of your legal conclusions.

The second problem, restatement of the facts, usually occurs because you haven't adequately thought through your answer. While you are writing a condensed version of the facts, you have time to think about what conclusions you are going to reach. But the reader is forced mentally to cut and paste your answer in order to connect facts with law and conclusions. Exactly how the facts lead to the conclusions (under the applicable legal theories) is a secret you have failed to divulge.

The third problem, juxtaposition, usually occurs because you have left out a connection that probably seems so obvious that it seems redundant to include it. Having carefully analyzed the problem and having reasoned your way to solid conclusions, you simply state the facts, the law, and the conclusions. In your own mind the connections are painfully obvious, but the reader wants to see you make them.

Incomplete Reasoning

Failing to show explicitly all of the steps in your reasoning process results in another type of conclusory answer. This type of answer was illustrated in the section on "Adopting Premises." You will notice that in making inferences we often rely on premises that are "hidden" in the sense that, because they come readily to our mind, we assume that they are apparent to everyone and fail to mention them. This is probably the most prevalent error among otherwise first-rate student papers. The writer carefully connects facts and legal theories in his or her own mind, but then fails to make the connections explicit when writing the conclusion.

There is a strategy you can use that may prevent this type of conclusory answer. Avoid beginning your answer or any paragraph within your answer with a conclusion. Don't say "Fred is liable for a battery against Brian," and then proceed to justify that statement. Instead, state the issue in the form of a question or statement of a question. "The question is whether Fred is liable for a battery against Brian." Then go on to reason your way to a conclusion. When you write a conclusion rather than an issue at the beginning of a paragraph, you tend to think of the conclusion as self-evident. After all, it's right there in black and white (depending on the color of ink you use). On the other hand, when you begin with a statement of issue and you know it is wise to end with a conclusion, you are faced with a great space in between, which you feel obliged to fill with something. If you can fill that void with an analysis of the facts and their connections to legal theory, you will be well on your way to justifying your conclusion.

Failure to Make Legal Principles Clear

One final way in which conclusory answers are sometimes written is through a failure to indicate the legal principles that are being applied to the facts in order to reach a conclusion. Given the facts and the conclusions, the reader who is knowledgeable can probably infer the legal principles used. However, it is unlikely that the reader will feel impelled to do so. After all, you're asking the reader to make your argument for you. Consider again the altercation between Brian and Fred the clergyman. Now look at the following answer.

> Brian has a cause of action in assault against Fred. All of the elements of assault are present. Fred swung at Brian; Brian ducked. Prior to this, Brian had told Fred not to touch him. Even though Fred is a clergyman, he would not be privileged to beat a demon out of Brian.

The writer has correctly identified all of the pertinent facts and has reached the "right" answer. In this student's mind, the thought of assault probably led to a comparison of the facts against a mental checklist of the elements of assault. However, when writing the answer, the student failed to make clear the elements in that checklist.

One strategy that can be used to avoid leaving out the legal theory when writing your answer is to follow the statement of an issue with the legal theory that you will be applying in that paragraph. One organizational approach is called IRAC—issue, rule, application, conclusion. (We will be discussing this in more detail in Chapter 3.) You may find that following a checklist can be useful to ensure that you include all of the parts necessary to support your conclusion. For example, consider the way this paragraph begins.

The issue is whether Brian has a cause of action in assault against Fred. Assault is an intentional, unprivileged, unconsented act that causes reasonable apprehension of an imminent touching.

The paragraph would then go on to show how the facts indicate the presence or absence of the elements of an assault. It would, of course, end with a conclusion about whether there was an assault.

LEGAL OVERKILL

The final instruction of the California Bar Examiners that we need to consider is addressed to the overzealous student.

Although your answer should be complete, you should not volunteer information or discuss legal doctrines that are not necessary or pertinent to the solution of the problem.

This instruction is quite simple. It tells you to answer the question and then stop. This is easy to say, but hard to do, particularly on law examinations. The problem is that you have learned so much information, absorbed so many legal principles, that you want to display all of your knowledge in one place. Unfortunately, this desire runs directly counter to the need to demonstrate your ability to discern the principles on which the case turns. If you tell a reader everything you know, you have shown that reader that you do not know how to separate the wheat from the chaff. (See Chapter 8 on clichés.)

There is no rule about how long an answer should be, or which principles it should contain. Some questions are limited by the examiner. "Discuss what liability, if any, Fred has to Brian." Others end only with "Discuss." The strategy you use must reflect the essential requirement that you discuss all issues raised in the question. Try to be complete. Careful organization will ensure that you have time enough to discuss all issues you identify.

CONCLUSION

We wish we could end this chapter with a more substantial legal strategy. It is always nice to have a socko finish. However, if you follow the specific examination-writing techniques in the next chapter, if you read the sample answers in Chapter 9, and if you write some practice answers for the questions we have provided, you will find that you are so busy doing the right things that you do not have time to volunteer information or discuss unnecessary legal doctrines. Or so we hope.

CHAPTER THREE
Writing an Answer
to a Law Examination

INTRODUCTION

In Chapter 2 we dealt with strategies for legal persuasion. We examined what the California Bar Examiners thought a good answer should contain, and tried to translate their precepts into some strategies that we could apply in preparing to write. In this chapter we examine the writing process as a whole, demonstrating specific techniques you can use to write an answer to an examination question or to answer a legal problem in a writing class. Our emphasis here is on what you can do when the moment of truth (or artful prevarication) comes and you are faced with a real question and a strict time limit. To illustrate the technique we recommend, we have chosen a problem that we have used for students who have had no legal training at all. All of the "law" necessary for answering the problem is contained within the problem itself.

PROBLEM

Harry and Wanda were married in the state of Zembla on October 12, 1985. Harry worked as a door-to-door shoe salesman and Wanda was the vice president of Ace Electronics. Each of them deposited their salaries in their own personal accounts.

In 1987 Harry's father died, leaving Harry a piece of land in Zembla valued at $100,000. In 1988 Wanda's boyfriend, Fred, gave her title to a small villa in Buenos Aires valued at $125,000.

In 1989 Fred told Wanda that he had a hot tip on Zero Computers, Inc. He said that within two years it would go from $10 per share to $100 per share. Without Harry's knowledge, Wanda went to the Second National Bank and obtained a loan for $10,000 with which she bought a thousand shares of Zero stock. The stock certificates listed Wanda and Harry as co-owners.

For two years Zero stock did magnificently, paying large dividends and rising steadily in value. Wanda used the $3,000 that she received in dividends to reduce the amount owed Second National to $7,000. Unfortunately, in 1992 it was discovered that the president of Zero had embezzled all of the company's funds, and the stock became worthless.

In 1993 Harry announced that he was going back to college to become an English professor. Horrified at the thought, Wanda decided to leave him. She went to her friend Claude, who was the president of the Valley Bank, and told him that she needed $10,000 to leave Harry. Claude advised her that the bank would not lend her the money for that purpose, but if she said that she wanted a home-improvement loan, she could get the money. She did just that. Unbeknownst to either Claude or Wanda, Harry's best friend Sam overheard the conversation.

Wanda took the $10,000, as well as all of the money she had in her personal account, and left for Buenos Aires with Fred. Undeterred, Harry quit his shoe-selling job that day, receiving his final check. He then took a job as a teaching assistant and began his studies at the university.

It is now 1994, and both the Second National Bank and the Valley Bank want to be paid. Harry has his land (now worth $150,000), $4,000 in earnings that he made as a shoe salesman, and $2,000 he has saved from his job as a teaching assistant. Both banks have sued Harry for their money, because it is impossible to find Wanda.

Harry has come to you to find out what his liabilities are under Zembla law. He wants to know specifically whether

a) he will have to pay all or part of the loan from Second National Bank, and
b) whether he will have to pay all or part of the loan from Valley Bank.

Discuss Harry's specific liabilities.

Zembla is a community-property state that has the following laws:

1. All property that is acquired during a marriage is community property. *Exception.* Any property that is acquired through a gift or inheritance is the separate property of the spouse who acquired it.
2. If the spouses have separated with the intention of permanently living apart, their earnings after the separation are the separate property of each spouse.
3. Either spouse may incur community debts and liabilities without the other's knowledge or consent, provided that the person incurring the debt or liability intends to benefit the community (husband and wife).
4. The separate property of each spouse is not considered when determining each spouse's liability for community debts.

Although the question looks fairly complicated at first reading, the issues are clear and the conclusion apparent and probable. After we give you a summary of the problem, we will go through it step-by-step, as you would in answering the question.

First, there are two loans outstanding: the one to Second National Bank for the stock, and the one to Valley Bank for Wanda's getaway. Two of the major issues, then, will be whether Harry has any liability for either of the two loans.

Then, if Harry is liable for either loan, there is the question of which of his assets can be taken by a bank to satisfy the debt. He has $4,000 earned before Wanda left, $2,000 earned after she left, and a piece of property worth $150,000, which he inherited.

PRE-WRITING/QUESTION ANALYSIS TECHNIQUE

You have just been given the problem and told that you have one hour in which to organize and write a coherent discussion of Harry's liabilities to the banks. Let us examine, step-by-step, how you would go through the writing process—analyzing, organizing, and writing your answer.

Identifying Relevant Facts

Obviously, the first thing that you must do is read the problem. However, you may waste a great deal of time if you try to extract all of the pertinent facts the first time through. Rather, you should read through the question first so that you have a general idea of what the facts are. Then, you should carefully read the instruction contained in the question. In our example you are given a very specific instruction—discuss whether Harry must pay *all* or *part* of the two different loans. In other questions you might simply be told to "Write a memo on . . . ," or "Discuss" something in the instructions. (Note that when teachers use the word "memo" in the context of an examination question, they usually do not mean anything more than a well-organized discussion. In Chapter 4, we discuss the intra-office memo and the memorandum of points and authorities.)

If you had tried to extract all of the pertinent facts on your first reading, you would have wasted time, because the instructions tell you that only certain issues are to be discussed. You might, for instance, have spent some time attempting to figure out whether Claude, the bank president, would be responsible for paying any of the loan, or whether the president of Zero Computer has any responsibility to the stockholders. But the instructions in the question restrict your area of inquiry, and you need only look for the facts that are pertinent to a discussion of what Harry might owe the banks. Thus, your techniques should be to read the question very rapidly, then read the instructions to learn whether your inquiry is to be restricted to certain parties or actions, and then go back to extract the pertinent facts.

Flagging the Facts

For some people, the best way to remember the facts that seem to "trigger" legal issues is to underline them or highlight them with a colored pen. Then, as they look at the question again, all the pertinent facts stand out. However, for many people—and we are among this group—neither highlighting nor underlining works because of our tendency to emphasize everything. When highlighting addicts get finished, they usually have colored the entire page. Indeed, so little is left uncolored that it is the uncolored, irrelevant material that stands out. The same is true for inveterate underliners. Consequently, highlighting addicts and inveterate underliners should use another method in exams.

As you go through the hypothetical situation, jot down on a separate piece of paper (or in the margin) the pertinent facts. (Remember, as we said in Chapter 2, facts become pertinent only in the light of a legal theory.) Do not write them out completely; just use key words that are sufficient to recall the facts to your mind. Writing down a fact is also a good way to be sure it has penetrated your consciousness. Too often underlining is almost a reflex action, and the underlined fact never enters your mind.

Brainstorming the Issues

After you have either underlined or listed all of the pertinent facts, note each of the possible issues that the fact raises. If a fact raises more than one issue, write all of the issues down. This is no time for censoring—let your mind take you where it will. Write down every single issue that pops into your head, even if you are not sure that it is appropriate. This process sometimes results in issues that are hidden in the facts popping into your mind. While the instructions in the question and the legal theories that you know (or have been given, as in this problem) help you to select the pertinent facts, the facts themselves will often suggest further issues.

All of this may seem terribly irrational and unlawyerlike. After all, we have been stressing the importance of logic, order, and organization in the previous chapters. In fact, we plan to spend a great deal more time stressing these concepts in later chapters. But there is a time to give your mind and imagination a chance to work on legal problems, and at this pre-writing stage of answering a legal question, you should do just that. Imagine the possibilities.

Defining the Possible Controversies

Legal questions almost invariably involve adversaries. For instance, in our problem each of the two banks will be trying to get their money from one or more of Harry's assets.

A straightforward way to proceed is simply to list the potential adversaries and fill in the controversies below them. In our example you would wind up with a list looking like this.

Second v Harry

—issue: was the liability incurred with the intention of benefiting the community?
—issue: what is the status of Harry's land? ($150,000)
  —if gift, no community property
  —if separate property, not liable for community debts
—issue: status of shoe earnings? ($4,000)
  —all property acquired during marriage is community property
  —community property—may be liable depending on whether liability incurred to benefit community
—issue: status of teaching assistant earnings? ($2,000)
  —is the money community property?
  —have they separated with the intention of permanently living apart? If so, separate property.
  —if separate property, no liability here.

Valley v Harry

—issue: was the liability incurred with the intention of benefiting the community?
—status of land?
—status of shoe earnings?
—status of T.A. earnings?

Outlining

After you have identified all of the parties and all of the pertinent legal issues along with the rules that you will need to address those issues, your next job is to organize the materials. Your first reaction to this suggestion might be that you damn well don't have enough time to start organizing if you have spent all of this time reading the problem and extracting the vital facts and issues. The simple answer, however, is that you cannot afford the luxury of not organizing.

Assume for a moment that you were faced with your bar examination and had an hour in which to write an answer to our practice problem. If you had done everything we have suggested to this point, almost ten minutes would have elapsed. If you spend another five minutes organizing your answer, you will have forty minutes to write and another five minutes to proofread what you have written. This may seem like utter insanity to you. After all, you might well think, with only sixty minutes to answer the question, and with so many things to be said, every minute has to be used for writing. Wrong.

In class after class that we have taught, we have asked students to experiment. In the first part of the experiment they spend no more than five minutes preparing to write and then spend the rest of their time writing an answer. In the second part of the experiment, students do not write until at least fifteen minutes have passed. Invariably students write more when they have spent fifteen minutes planning what they are going to write than when they spend only five minutes preparing. Why? That's easy. When you know where you are going, you don't make a lot of false starts and have to begin again or explain away what you previously said. Nor do you have to search for the next idea. It is all there. Like a road map, your outline guides you directly to where you have to go. Examine, for example, this road-map outline for our sample problem. Notice that the sequence in which things are to be discussed is clear.

1. issue: Harry's liability to the Second National Bank.
2. issue: Harry's liability to Valley Bank.
3. issue: The status of Harry's inherited property.
4. issue: The status of Harry's $4,000.
5. issue: The status of Harry's $2,000.

Perhaps the importance of outlining can be brought home most forcefully if we examine a student answer to our problem.

> Issues in this case are whether Harry is liable to pay all or part of a loan from Second National Bank, and whether he is liable for the loan from Valley Bank.
>
> Harry and Wanda were legally married in the state of Zembla. During this marriage both partners worked and deposited their salaries into personal accounts. Because Zembla is a community-property state and the law says that "all property acquired during a marriage is presumed to be community property," their separate bank accounts are presumed to be community property.
>
> Also during the marriage, Harry acquired land in Zembla left to him by his father, who had died. Wanda also received a gift valued at $125,000. This property was not community property because of the exception to the rule, which states that any property that is acquired through a gift or inheritance is the separate property of the spouse who acquired it.
>
> Sometime later, Wanda borrowed $10,000 from the Second National Bank to buy stock. She did this because Fred had given her a "hot tip" and he had said the stock would rise considerably. Because the wife can be manager of community property and can incur community debts and liabilities without the husband's knowledge or consent provided that she intends to benefit the community, and because Wanda bought the stock certificates and listed herself and Harry as co-owners, the loan to the bank would be considered community property. Also, the dividend from the stock went to pay some of the loan to Second National Bank.
>
> Under the pretense of a home-improvement loan, Wanda receives $10,000 and then leaves for Buenos Aires. She takes her money and the $10,000 and leaves with her boyfriend. Thus, it is assumed she leaves permanently. Therefore, this loan is not community property but separate because the law states that if the spouses have separated with the intention of permanently living apart, their earnings are the separate property of each spouse. Also, this loan was not intended to benefit the community, and therefore, it cannot be community property.

Therefore, the loan from . . . (at this point the student ran out of time).

While most of the issues have been addressed, the order in which they were considered did not allow this student to explain Harry's liability clearly. If you have carefully read Chapters 1 and 2, you will be able to identify almost every major error we have mentioned, all in this one paper. The student who wrote this paper was certainly not stupid. However, he did panic when faced with what he saw as a fairly complex fact pattern. You can see without difficulty the way in which this paper was organized. The student merely followed the question, paragraph by paragraph, and made what he could of the facts. It is not until the last sentence of the last paragraph that it begins to dawn on him that there is a method for dealing with these facts that would allow him to consider the issues in an orderly fashion. Let us see if we can discover this method.

The initial analysis showed two banks to which Harry might owe money, and three portions of property that the banks might be able to get. But before you can decide which portions of property are liable for community debts, you have to decide *if* there are community debts. Therefore, you will have to discuss the debts first.

Relationships among Controversies.   With our student example in mind, you should be able to understand clearly the first rule we want to suggest for organization. Although there may be more than one logical order in which to discuss the controversies, there will be some sequences that are clearly illogical. For instance, in our problem it would be inappropriate to decide which of the assets must be used to pay the Valley Bank before deciding whether Harry has any liability to the bank at all. Certainly you could say that *if* he were liable, *then* this particular asset would be used. Then you could go on and do the same for the Second National Bank. But that approach would consume a great deal of time and show an inability to determine what issues are crucial.

What we are saying, of course, is that sometimes by deciding one issue you simplify your task in deciding the rest. Thus, where one determination is the foundation on which another rests (for instance, in our problem the liability of Harry's assets depends first on whether either of the debts is a community obligation), you should *decide the foundation question first.*

Arranging the Issues in Order.   When you have decided which issues require discussion, you can then decide on the order in which you are going to discuss them. Quite often, a chronological discussion is easiest and perfectly adequate. However, this does not mean that you discuss every item that you were given in the fact pattern in the order in which it was given. (Remember the student paper we considered in which every single fact was discussed in the order given.) Rather, when you know what the issues are and how they are logically related to one another, you can decide which ones to discuss first. For instance, in our problem we decided that the question of whether there was any liability to a bank had to be discussed before we talked about the liability of a particular asset. The major headings then could look like this.

  I. Introduction
 II. Is Harry liable to Second? (probably)
III. Is Harry liable to Valley? (no)
 IV. Which of Harry's assets is liable for the $7,000?
     A. lot? (no)
     B. savings from shoe job? (yes)
     C. savings from T.A. stipend? (probably not)

As you can see, this outline follows a chronological order. Because the loan from Second was made before the loan from Valley, that is considered first. The assets are also considered in the order of acquisition.

There are, of course, other possible orders in which the issues could have been outlined. For instance, you might have organized your outline with III and IV in the above example reversed.

  I. Introduction
 II. Is Harry liable to Second? (probably)
III. If so, which of Harry's assets is liable for the $7,000?
     A. lot? (no)
     B. shoe earnings? (yes)
     C. T.A. earnings? (probably not)
 IV. Is Harry liable to Valley? (no)
  V. If so, which of assets?
     A. lot? (no)
     B. shoe earnings? (yes)

Now, having decided whether Harry was liable for the loan to Second, you could have gone on to discuss which of his assets would be liable for that debt and, then, whether there was any liability to Valley. This strategy would have allowed you to cover yourself by saying that *if* a court found that the loan from Valley *was* made for community purposes (a highly unlikely construction), then the liability of Harry's assets would be the same as under the analysis for Second.

Ending Each Section with a Conclusion. There is one important element in the last outlines we have looked at. In every case you should indicate how each controversy would be resolved. You must decide each of the issues that you consider. It is far more important that you reach a logical conclusion than that you reach the "right" conclusion.

If you know what conclusion you are going to reach before you start writing, you will find that it is much easier to write concise, well-reasoned paragraphs.

Checking the Outline for Balance. As we mentioned in both Chapters 1 and 2, you must be sure that your answer is not one-sided, that you consider the possible arguments that will be used by your opponent. The time to balance your argument is when you are making your outline. As you match facts with legal theories, you will undoubtedly discover facts that are equivocal (ones that could be used on either side of the argument) or fact patterns that are incomplete (ones that leave you to draw inferences to reach any legal conclusion).

In our problem we can see that the fact that "the stock certificates listed Wanda and Harry as co-owners" is not enough to decide whether Wanda intended the purchase of stock to benefit the community. Certainly, you could argue that by putting the certificates in both their names she intended that both of them benefit from the hoped-for increase in the price of the stock. On the other hand, because Harry did not know of the stock purchase, it might be irrelevant that the certificates listed him as a co-owner. Wanda, as possible manager of the community, might well sell the stock—after it increased in value—without Harry's knowledge. If that were the case, it could be said that she did not intend to benefit the community. Of course, as we discussed earlier, because this inference requires an additional assumption (that Wanda would later sell the stock without telling Harry), it is less probable than the other inference. What is vital, however, is that you consider the other side when making your outline and writing your answer.

IRAC. IRAC (pronounced "eye-rack") is an acronym for issue, rule, application, conclusion. As a mnemonic device, it is useful for remembering that each of those four elements must be contained in every paragraph of a law answer. While it is best not to be too mechanical in your use of IRAC, you can at least go over your outline with this checklist in mind to be sure that you have not left any of these elements out.

I   State the *issue* explicitly.

R   Refer to the *rule* of law.

A   You have to *apply* the rules to the facts in a complete analytical discussion. *This is the most important step.*

C   Come to a *conclusion* after your discussion of an issue.

This mnemonic device is often helpful in making sure you have the necessary ingredients in your answer.

Miscellaneous Hints for Outlining.   We have a few more suggestions for outlining that we offer under the categories of "client consciousness," direction, and time.

In many questions you are asked to represent one or the other of the parties. What this means for outlining is that you must keep this person's perspective in mind when you are analyzing and putting together your arguments. While you must consider both sides of the argument when you are given such as assignment, your emphasis should be on your "client's" interests.

To be sure of your direction, you should have your outline complete before you begin to write. That probably sounds obvious, but the path to mediocre exams is strewn with half-written outlines. You start out with the best intentions and, as you begin to outline, everything you want to say falls into place in your mind. So you begin to write. After you are well along in your answer, however, you become so enmeshed in your arguments that you forget where it was you intended to go. Then you have to sit and think about what to write next, negating all the beneficial effects of having written part of an outline.

One way of being sure that you get all the benefits of organizing and outlining is to set for yourself an arbitrary time before which you will not begin to write your answer. For a question of about an hour we suggest at least ten to fifteen minutes. Refuse to write a single word of your draft before that time has passed. Then stick to that decision. Many students have recounted how, having finished their outline before our allotted fifteen minutes, they simply sat and thought. During the time they were thinking, new points, ideas, or issues came to mind. They then incorporated these new ideas into the outline, and wrote a better answer than they would have before the additional thinking was done.

WRITING THE ANSWER

We have already talked extensively about the strategy employed in writing law answers. We must now consider the techniques to employ in writing those answers. All of these techniques should be considered in the light of your overall persuasive strategy and not as magical "rules" that will automatically lead to success.

Overall Techniques

You may remember Uncle Melvin from Chapter 2. He is somewhat cantankerous and insists that you explain things step-by-step and without using any big words. If you keep his needs in mind, you may avoid inflated diction, hidden assumptions, and failures to state explicitly the legal principles you are using.

Another technique that seems to be useful in writing law answers directed toward Uncle Melvin is to try to be conscious of the words "because," "therefore," and "since." When you practice writing an answer, be sure that every time you reach a conclusion there is a "because," or "since" that leads your reader from the facts to the law, and a "therefore" that leads from the law to a conclusion. Sometimes, when you think of the words "because," or "therefore" in the sentences, what you see before you doesn't make sense. That means you have tried to substitute a word for a logical flow of ideas. You must go back and straighten out your ideas, because a logical transition is not enough to make a logical argument.

Introduction

The introduction in a law answer need not be as extensive as the introduction in other types of essays. However, you should introduce the issues so that your answer does not appear to start in the middle of nowhere. Consider this example.

> The issues in this case are how much of Wanda's incurred debt Harry is liable for under Zembla law and how much of his net worth is exempt from liability.

In this very brief introduction, the student has set up the major issues in the case and the order in which he is going to discuss them. That is all you need to do in an introduction to a law answer.

The Body of the Answer

We can begin to look at the body of an answer by looking first at a single paragraph within the body.

> The next issue is whether the $4,000 Harry earned as a shoe salesman must go to the Second National Bank. Zembla law states that for Harry's earnings to be separate property, he and Wanda must have separated with the intention of permanently living apart. But Harry and Wanda did not split up until Harry quit being a shoe salesman to become an English teacher. Because there was no separation until after Harry had earned the $4,000 as a shoe salesman, we must conclude that the money will not be considered separate property. Instead, it will be considered community property and will be used toward the remaining $7,000 owed Second National Bank.

Notice that in this paragraph the only issue that the student is considering is whether the $4,000 must go to the Second National Bank for the $7,000 liability. Here a single subissue is discussed. It is important to remember that the discussion has to be complete. Remember the IRAC formula. You need to introduce the issue, cite the Zemblan law, apply the law to the facts, and reach a conclusion. The next section of the answer will be a consideration of whether the $2,000 earned as a teaching assistant must be used for the debt.

In this example, discussions of issues are brief and require only a single paragraph. If an issue requires more discussion, however, you will probably need to break your discussion into several paragraphs to follow our suggestion of keeping paragraphs short.

Conclusion

Like the introduction, the conclusion in a law answer should occupy very little space. Indeed, if you are running out of time and are faced with a choice between adequately discussing an issue and including a conclusion, your choice should be clear: forget about the conclusion. However, if you do have time for a conclusion, it should be just a brief answer to the interrogatory posed in the question itself. Consider this conclusion.

Under Zembla law Harry will be liable to Second National Bank alone and only for the $4,000 of community property.

While we would normally rail against one-sentence paragraphs, this one is fine for the purpose of concluding a law exam answer.

Editing/Proofreading

Sometimes the toughest thing to do after you have finished writing an answer is to look at the bloody thing again. However, it does give you an opportunity to correct many writing errors that would otherwise lower the value of your paper in the estimation of the reader or even keep you from being understood at all. While we talk in Chapter 7 about the specific errors that are most commonly made, it is important for you to remember, as a matter of technique, that you must save a few minutes to proofread your answer.

While you are doing this, you might try to say every word that you have written (under your breath, of course). You might also try to keep the words "because," "since," and "therefore" in mind again, so that you stand a chance of discovering any possible omissions of logical steps.

SAMPLE ANSWER

There is a great temptation among authors to include a "perfect" sample answer. Having written the question, and having all the time in the world, we could probably write such an answer (or at least a passing answer). However, we have decided instead to include an actual student answer as representative of what can be expected in a timed, one-hour examination.

The issues in this case are how much of Wanda's incurred debt Harry is liable for under Zembla law, and how much of his worth is exempt from liability.

Second National Bank may have a cause of action against Harry to collect the remaining $7,000 due on the loan that Wanda made to purchase Zero Computer stock. However, Harry was unaware that Wanda borrowed the money. Even so, Zembla law states that either spouse may incur community debts without the knowledge or consent of the other spouse provided she intends to benefit the community.

Harry may claim that there was no intention to benefit the community because he didn't even know about the transaction. However, since Wanda listed Harry as co-owner of the stock, he would benefit from any increase in Zero's value whether or not he knew of the stock. Because Wanda showed her intent to benefit the community by making Harry co-owner, Harry is obligated to pay the remaining debt.

However, Zembla law also states that the separate property of each spouse is not liable for community debts. Thus, it is necessary to consider the status of each of Harry's three assets.

The first asset to be considered is the land Harry inherited from his father during his marriage to Wanda. According to Zembla law, property acquired during a marriage is presumed to be community property *unless* it was acquired through a gift or inheritance. Because Harry clearly inherited the land, it would be considered separate property. Furthermore, because Zembla law states that separate property is not liable for community debts, Second National cannot look to Harry's land to satisfy the $7,000 debt.

The second asset belonging to Harry that the Second National Bank will look to is the $4,000 in earnings that Harry made as a shoe salesman. Zembla law states that for Harry's earnings to be considered separate property, he and Wanda must have separated with the intention of permanently living apart. But Harry and Wanda did not split up until Harry quit his job as a shoe salesman to become an English teacher. Because there was no separation until after Harry had earned the $4,000, we must conclude that the money will not be considered separate property and *will* be used toward the remaining $7,000 owed Second National Bank.

The last of Harry's assets to be considered is the $2,000 he earned as a teaching assistant after Wanda left for Buenos Aires. Under Zembla law, earnings made after an intention to separate permanently are considered separate property. The issue is whether the intent was to live apart permanently. The facts are not explicit, but since Wanda has not been heard from, and since it is apparently impossible to find her, it is reasonable to assume that she has intended to separate from Harry permanently. Thus, Second National Bank cannot seize the $2,000 because separate property is not liable for community debts.

The next issue is whether Harry is liable to Valley Bank for the $10,000 "home improvement" loan taken out by Wanda shortly before she left. Although under Zembla law, Wanda could incur community debts, she must intend to benefit the community. If it were in fact a loan for home improvement, Harry would be liable. However, since Wanda told Claude that she wanted the money to leave Harry, and since Harry's friend, Sam, overheard it and can verify it, it is clear that her intent was to break up the community rather than benefit it. Because only those debts incurred to benefit the community are community debts, Harry would not be liable to Valley Bank.

As you can see, the answer is not perfect. However, it is clearly organized and stated directly. The discussions are not extensive, but there is an application of the law to the facts. Logical transitions help lead the reader through the reasoning process. Issues, rules, application, and conclusions are presented in an orderly way. Overall, this is a pretty good paper, and you can see how it results from the pre-writing process. You should reread this paper to get a more concrete idea of some of the things we have been talking about.

CONCLUSION

It would be nice to think that after reading a sample answer twice you are ready to go out and write perfect exam answers. It would also be nice to win the lottery. Neither is highly probable. But you can significantly improve your chances of writing good examination answers with a bit of diligence. First, you should be sure you thoroughly understand the principles in this and the previous chapter. Second, you should read some of the sample questions in Chapter 9, organize and write an answer, and then read the sample answer. Third, you should write answers to the sample questions we have provided in the Appendix. The more times you practice the strategies and techniques we recommend, the more they will become a part of the basic skills you bring to examinations. Then, no matter how difficult the question, you will be prepared to demonstrate all of your legal writing abilities properly.

CHAPTER FOUR
Writing Legal Memoranda

INTRODUCTION

In almost every law school in the country, students are required to do three kinds of legal writing assignments. They must write essay examination answers, memoranda, and briefs. We have already talked about how to write answers to examination questions. Now we are going to apply the techniques you have learned in previous chapters to the task of writing longer and more formal documents. In this chapter we will focus on the legal memorandum.

The term "memoranda" may refer to two types of documents. One is called the "intraoffice memorandum" or the "office memorandum." A second type of memorandum is called the "memorandum of points and authorities" or "memorandum of law." The memorandum of law is essentially a minibrief. It is usually used in support of a motion or argument that is being made before a court. As with any document that is to be presented to a court, when you are in practice you will check the rules of your local court to determine when a memorandum of law is required and what the appropriate form is. In those instances where no form is provided, you can use the generic format included in the next section of this chapter.

The office memorandum, which some people simply refer to as a memo, is the most common exercise used in law school writing classes. The reason it is assigned so commonly is that most new law graduates, when they get their first job, will have to turn out many memos. Indeed, if you are lucky enough to get a summer law job while in law school, you will undoubtedly be producing memos for your supervisor.

A memo is a researched and written answer to one or more legal questions. The purpose of having a memo written is to obtain a highly accurate prediction of the probable outcome of any future hearing or court proceeding based on the facts that have been provided to the memo writer. The distinguishing feature of an office memo is its objectivity. The memo must emphasize both the strengths and weaknesses in the clients' and the opposing parties' positions. It always has some sort of conclusion and often recommends the most favorable strategy for the client involved.

FORMAT

In some ways, the format of a memorandum is the least important aspect of it. Students, however, often waste an enormous amount of time trying to figure out what the document should look like. For memoranda, there is no set format. It varies from law office to law office, depending on the filing system that office uses and various other factors. While we will offer a suggested format below, you must understand that it is only a suggestion. What your memo should look like will depend on your instructor or the office in which you are working.

Office Memoranda

As with memos in any field, legal memoranda begin with a standard format.

date:
to:
from:
re:

While "to" and "from" are self-explanatory, the "re" line needs a bit of explanation. Many offices file and cross-file memoranda so that the same point is not researched time after time by different people. In those offices the "re" line may have certain identifying letters or numbers that are peculiar to the internal filing system of the firm. If the office in which you are working does not have a system, a good idea is to attempt a "re" line that would fit some place in the West Key Number Index System. That is, you should decide what words or phrases best describe the legal issue involved. The date section, while self-explanatory, has a very important purpose. In addition to telling the person for whom you wrote the memo when it was done, it allows research to be used again in the future. That is, someone who later picks up your memo will be able to see how current it is. By simply researching the topic from the date of your memo to the present, others can use your work for their own tasks.

The body of the memo typically contains the following elements.

issue:

summary of conclusion:

facts:

discussion:

conclusion:

The issue should be framed precisely and it must be placed in the context of the relevant theory of law. Before writing a memo, you must attempt to formulate the proper question. If you are unfamiliar with the area of law involved, however, you will first need to do some basic research. You cannot correctly formulate a question until you have gained some familiarity with the area. You must be able to place the question within a larger context of some area of the law. For instance, you may have a tort question involving negligence and that subarea of negligence known as proximate cause. Until you know that this is the area that you are to be concerned with, you are unprepared to formulate a question properly. Thus, it is important for you to follow our suggestions for research and analysis before formulating the issue.

Next will come a summary of the conclusion. A detailed and fully explained conclusion usually follows the discussion, but the summary allows for quick reference to an abstract of the conclusion.

The facts section should be a concise, accurate, and organized presentation of the facts that led to the legal question discussed in your memo. The section should begin with a clause or sentence that puts the facts into some context. The reader must be provided with the larger picture, of which these facts are only a portion. Sometimes, the facts will be the entire picture. Your job is to make sure the picture is clear.

In the discussion section, you take the authority that you have found through your research and apply it to the facts you have been provided. In doing so, your purpose is to come up with the *strengths* and *weaknesses* of your client's position. It is not your purpose to *argue* your client's position. In this section you state what the law is so that the person reading the memo will later be able to use it for negotiation, client advice, or preparation for litigation.

The conclusion is a probability statement. In it you make a prediction as to what a court will do based on the facts that have been presented to you. The conclusion is the result of your legal research and is supported by the discussion section that precedes it. In addition, you may be asked to make some suggestions as to potential strategies for a client based on the conclusion you have reached on the point of law involved.

Memorandum of Points and Authorities

As we mentioned at the beginning of the chapter, the Memorandum of Points and Authorities is a researched adversarial document—a minibrief—which is filed in support of a motion or argument. You must consult the rules of your local court to determine the appropriate format. We can describe a generic format, however, to give you an idea of the contents of this type of memorandum.

Title Page
Table of Contents
Table of Authorities
Introduction (or Summary of Conclusion)
Facts
Argument
Conclusion

The title page identifies the parties, case, and court involved. The table of contents is necessary because this may be a somewhat lengthy document and page references are important. The table of authorities lists cases referred to and any relevant statutes or regulations. The introduction provides background and presents the issue and summary of the argument. Facts are presented, followed by the argument itself. The argument will include references to the research undertaken to support it. Finally, the conclusion will be clearly stated.

WRITING THE MEMORANDUM

Pre-Writing

Purpose. The purpose of an office memo is to obtain a highly accurate prediction of the probable outcome of any future hearing or court proceeding involving the facts and issues discussed in the memo. The distinguishing feature of the memo is its objectivity. You must remember that it is not an advocacy document. You must emphasize the strengths and weaknesses of the positions of both your client and the opposing party.

The secondary purpose of a memo (and it is very much secondary) is to record your research for future use. This secondary purpose is worth mentioning only because you may otherwise be tempted to take writing shortcuts based on the knowledge that you and your current audience have. If you assume too much in writing the memo, its later usefulness will be limited. In fact, to the extent that you are in a large office where the memo may pass through several hands, including those of some who are not familiar with this particular case, your assumptions may limit the usefulness of the memo for other persons.

Audience. When you write an office memo, you have one of the most clearly defined audiences you will ever have for any writing task. In general, you are writing a memo for a specific partner or other supervisor who has asked you to research some point of law. When you are writing a memo in law school, it is for a hypothetical partner who has given you exactly the same task. The expectations of both are exactly the same. Both expect a carefully researched, balanced treatment of the issue presented.

Voice.   Objectivity is the hallmark of an office memo. Because its purpose is to weigh the law on both sides, your voice should be both balanced and clinically detached. You should not use adjectives that characterize facts or rules of law. Nor should you use any of the devices for emphasis that we discuss later in explaining how to argue in a brief. Rather, you should attempt as a lawyer to speak like a scientist. That is, you describe facts and laws and make high-probability inferences as to the outcome that would be reached under applicable law using this set of facts. The most egregious error you can make, in voice, is to have your memo sound like an argument. The moment you begin to sound argumentative, the reader begins to question whether you have looked carefully at both sides of the issue presented. If the reader loses confidence in the writer, the memo will be useless. The reader will feel obliged to have someone else redo the work, or to read carefully and completely all of the cases involved. Thus, it is impossible to overstress the importance of a balanced, objective voice in the memo.

Analysis.   In analyzing a fact situation for writing an office memo, you must integrate both analysis and research. Your initial analysis will lead you to do certain research. Your research will lead you to new questions that will require further analysis. That further analysis may again require more research. In effect, there is a feedback loop in which analysis leads to research, which leads to further analysis with further research, which leads, finally, to the analysis you will be using in the memo itself. To make the most effective use of your research and analysis, you must incorporate brainstorming, organizing, and outlining into the feedback loop. We will first explain the analysis/research feedback loop and then examine how the other processes are essential parts of it.

We will assume that you have been given a fact-based problem to research. What that means is that you do not have a predefined, narrowly focused legal issue. Rather, you have a problem that is raised by some facts. The first step in the pre-writing process is to make a preliminary analysis of what legal categories your problem fits into. Start out with broad categories and terms that may need definition. You will find that your research at this point may include such things as legal dictionaries and legal encyclopedias. The dictionaries give you preliminary definitions for terms you do not understand. The encyclopedias, as well as statutory indices or schematics—such as those contained in the West Key Number indices—provide overall pictures of the way the law is broken down. They may not provide definitive answers for your problem, but they will give you an idea of where your problem fits in the legal scheme of things.

The next step in this preliminary analysis is to reformulate the problem. You must determine what legal issues are raised by the facts. As part of your initial research, you may have discovered that you have too few facts, or facts that are ambiguous. In either event, you know that you will need to find additional facts, if that is possible. In the law school setting, that is rarely possible. In the law office setting, you may be able to obtain the facts from the person who assigned the memo or from the client. In other instances, there will simply be no way of ascertaining the facts. When that is the case, you will know as part of your analysis that you are going to have to make explicit assumptions about some of the facts. In making those assumptions, you will, of course, do multiple analyses. Each of the potential factual settings will lead to a different analysis, all of which must be contained in your memo. What should be clear thus far is that you may have two different types of "issues." That is, there are issues of fact that can be resolved by finding the necessary facts through questions, interviews, or other research means. Then there are legal questions. These legal questions are, of course, "issues" as we normally understand that term in law.

After you have identified the issues and eliminated whatever factual questions you could, you should brainstorm. In so doing, you may find it useful to go back to an index or an encyclopedia article to look at categories again in the hope that they may give you an idea. Alternatively, you may look at a leading case or two, simply to see if the discussions in those cases give you any new ideas. Your purpose is not, at the moment, to do complete research.

After you have brainstormed a bit, you are ready to do further research into your legal issues. The next step is to look for statutes that may control the issue involved in your fact situation. Naturally, if you find that the matter is controlled by statute, you will research the decisions under that statute to learn where you stand. If there is no statutory or constitutional material that covers your problem, you will next look for mandatory precedents.

In the process of looking for mandatory precedents (cases whose holdings must be followed in the jurisdiction in which you are arguing), you will engage in the search for analogies. What cases are closest, factually, to yours? What legal theories are discussed that could be applied to your case? If there is no mandatory precedent in your jurisdiction, you may have to look for persuasive precedents (cases that are well reasoned but do not have to be followed by the jurisdiction in which you are arguing).

In addition to making the analogy between your case and the other cases, you must do something else. You must abstract the legal principle that the court is using in order to determine whether the reasoning behind the principle is applicable in your situation. In addition, you may need to look at a number of decisions in your own jurisdiction, none of which are precisely on point or mandatory precedent in your case. You may discover that the synthesis of a series of applicable principles will result in a new principle to be applied in your case. As you go through the cases, you may also discover new theories that could apply to your fact situation. You will, of course, note these.

The most common student error in the pre-writing stage of the office memo is to do prodigious amounts of unfocused research. One case leads to another. The amount of law that a student (or any lawyer) knows is always vastly overshadowed by the amount of unknown law. Consequently, days can be spent researching a very simple point simply because the cases lead to one another in an almost unbroken series of ripples. But the research task is not, usually, to expose the outermost ripples. Rather, the job of researching the office memo is to find the rock at the bottom of the pond. The way to do this is by organizing and outlining.

Organizing.   The purpose of organizing your research is not to impose a structure on the mass of data you have accumulated. Rather, the task is to focus your current research through organizing the fruits of your earlier research as soon as you have gathered them. For many students, the research effort is an unbroken string of days sitting in a law library briefing cases onto a yellow pad. This is probably the least useful way of researching anything. Rather, every case you read should immediately be categorized into one of the potential issue areas involved in your memo. If the case relates to a single aspect of an issue, it should be categorized that way. If the case can be viewed in a number of different ways, it should be categorized in a number of different ways. As you do this, you should be making an outline showing where each case you read fits and how the cases relate to one another. Otherwise, you will wind up with sheaves of yellow note paper filled with useless notes.

In addition, as you categorize cases and put them into your outline, you will discover that you will have questions about some aspect of the case. Since you have just finished reading the case, it is available, and you can go back and check that aspect. Otherwise, you may find yourself rereading many cases.

As you are organizing cases, it is also helpful to use graphic devices. You may find, for instance, that you need a table to show which cases relate to which aspect of your problem. Keep updating the table as you go along so you always know where you are in your research. You may also need a time line to organize key cases chronologically so that you can see the development of a theory or the potential to develop a new theory. Finally, it may be useful to do lists of theories, with their elements, so that you have a checklist for research. Your basic task is to avoid reading the same cases repeatedly or going off into areas that have little relationship to your problem.

Outlining. While we have previously spoken about outlining as you go along, that is only one type of outlining. The other type of outlining is for your discussion section. To do this outline, which should probably be written in a skeletal form, you must know the logical relationship between the facts and the issues you have identified. It may be useful for you to begin with a flowchart, such as the one we discuss in the chapter on logic. This is a graphic device for determining whether you have covered all of the legal aspects of a given issue. Your outline for the discussion section of your memo will also show you what should be your topic sentences. As you review these you will discover any gaps in your knowledge. You can then go back through another analysis/research feedback loop to discover these facts.

In addition, you may discover that your outline simply does not make sense in places. If that is so, your analysis has been inadequate. To identify the inadequacies in your analysis, it is important that you make a skeletal outline, using topic sentences and references to the cases on which you plan to rely.

Another aspect that will become obvious from your skeletal outline is that on certain issues there are quite clearly two sides. Because you are doing a memo, rather than an advocacy document, you will want to be sure that your treatment is balanced. That is, you should not simply dismiss the legal authority that is opposed to your client's perceived interest. Instead, you should give it as much space as you give the authority that is in favor of your client's perceived interest. The same is true of counterarguments that could be made to the arguments that your client makes. It is of no benefit to the person for whom you are writing the memo to have a one-sided view of either of those. You should assume that your opponent has someone as smart as you (well, almost), working as hard as you, on this case. When your outline is complete, logical, and balanced, you are ready to begin writing.

Writing/Drafting

One of the unusual aspects of the memo is that the conclusion comes before the discussion. It is done this way so that those who ask for memos are not obliged to read through them or flip pages to see how it all comes out. By the time you have finished your outline, you will be able to write a succinct, clear conclusion. This conclusion, in effect, serves as an introduction to your discussion section. Thus, while we have emphasized the importance of an introduction and a conclusion in some kinds of writing, neither is necessary as part of the discussion section of your memo. What is vital is the use of signposts. You will be discussing both sides of various aspects of the issue. Because you are discussing both sides, it can be terribly confusing to the reader. The best way to avoid this confusion is to begin by telling the reader how many aspects there are and whether you will be discussing the pro and con together or separately. In most instances, it is not useful to separate the discussion section into that which supports your conclusion and that which does not. It is usually easier to discuss each aspect of the issue and include the pro and con in the same paragraph, or in separate paragraphs that follow one another. There are times, however, when it may be useful to simply divide the memo discussion into a pro and con section. Only experience and the guidance of your instructor will teach you when to do that.

Clarity and Style.   Your style in a memo is extremely important. When we discussed voice, we noted that you must have a "clinical" voice in your memo. Your reader must be assured that you are not advocating one side of the issue and in so doing ignoring the other side. One of the ways you can ensure this is through using more simple sentences than you might otherwise. Simple, declarative sentences do not lend themselves to hiding anything.

As we discuss later, there are ways of burying facts or uncomfortable pieces of law. None of them includes using a series of simple, declarative sentences. On the other hand, we recognize that this kind of writing can become boring for the reader and that some variation is required. Keep in mind, however, that if you start with simple sentences, even if you later rewrite to add variety, you will not fool yourself when drafting. What makes a memo clear is the writer's complete understanding of the subject matter about which he or she is writing. A lack of clarity simply reflects the writer's lack of understanding.

The next most common problem is the use of "legalese." Often, the two problems are related. A writer may not understand the meaning of a term that is being used in a number of decisions. Rather than look up the term and try to develop an understanding of it, the writer simply repeats it time after time. On the other hand, sometimes the writer may understand the terms, but he or she does not understand the relationships between ideas. When that occurs we usually see sentences such as, "problem X as it relates to Y . . . ," or "X with respect to Y. . . ." Both of these equivocations are sure signs that the writer does not understand, or has not been able to express an understanding of, the relationship between X and Y. If you find these or similar equivocations in your memo, go back and rewrite the sentences so that you make clear the relationship between X and Y. If you cannot do that, perhaps you need to do some more research.

Unity and Coherence.   When students have a problem with lack of unity or coherence, it is usually because they have failed to organize properly before beginning to write. The writer must create a hierarchical organization that shows which ideas and cases encompass which other ideas and cases. Otherwise, the discussion proves to be a series of discrete "points." These points are no more than a series of holdings in different cases cited by the student. How these cases all fit together to support the student's conclusion is left for the reader to decide. When this occurs, however, the reader's faith in the writer is so shaken that the reader is more likely to assign the research to someone else or read all of the cases to attempt to discern how they do fit together. If the reader is a professor or instructor, you may expect a low grade.

To ensure coherence, the same principles of transition that you use in any other form of legal writing should be used in the memo. Do not leave gaps the reader has to bridge with intuitive leaps. Instead, show the logical relationships between the parts of your paragraph. At the same time, be careful not to fool yourself. It is easy to substitute words such as "therefore," "consequently," "thus," "clearly," and "obviously" for the actual logical steps that lead up to them. Whenever you use one of these "logic markers," check what has gone before. If your reasoning does not lead inevitably to the conclusion that you have made, check your reasoning again. At times, of course, facts from the real world will not conform perfectly to logical sequences. In those instances, you may get some help from a logical transition. Do not, however, depend on them to replace solid logic.

Revising

As we noted earlier, the best way to revise is by asking yourself specific questions. Start by asking whether the issue is clearly identified. Much of your research has involved a constant reanalysis of the issues. After you have written your discussion section, you should examine your issue again. Do the answers in your conclusion respond unequivocally to the questions raised in your issue? If not, either the issue or the conclusion must be reformulated. Does the discussion provide an unbreakable link between the issue and the conclusion? If not, you must revise and rewrite.

Have any facts been left out? Re-examine your fact section in light of your issue and discussion sections. It is fairly common for memo writers to fail to update their fact sections. That is, having encountered some factual ambiguity and resolved it, they do not rewrite the fact section. If there is any fact used in your discussion section that does not appear in the fact section, add it. Conversely, if there are any facts that appear in your fact section that do not have any bearing on the discussion or issue, they should be removed. You should, of course, keep those that you put in solely to provide an adequate context for future audiences who are reading your memo.

Have you reached a logical conclusion that is fully supported in the discussion? Before writing, you checked your outline to be sure of the logic of your discussion. Many times, however, there are slips between the outline and the discussion itself. As you begin a paragraph with the topic sentence you intended to use all along, your thinking has already changed. As a result, the paragraph goes somewhere other than where the topic sentence suggested it should go. If you have written a number of these paragraphs, your conclusion may simply be unsupported by the discussion following it.

There is another way in which your conclusion may be unsupported. Because your conclusion embodies a prediction as to what a court or tribunal will do, you must be sure that this prediction is a high-probability inference that can be made from the authorities you have discussed. It is easy to convince yourself of the correctness of your client's position. It is also dangerous. Try rereading your discussion section as though you were your opponent. Does it still lead you to the conclusion you wrote? If not, perhaps you should express more uncertainty about your conclusion.

Ideally, you will leave enough time in your busy schedule to let your memo sit overnight before turning it in. If you can do that, reread it a couple of hours before it is due. Are your explanations still as clear as they seemed initially? If not, revise. Are your sentences predominantly simple and direct? If not, revise. Have you filled your discussion with legalese? If so, revise.

Editing

You should ruthlessly edit everything you write. For both law professors and practicing lawyers, there is too little time for all the things that we must read. None of us has the time to indulge in wordy, overwritten documents. Consequently, you should go through your memo with an eye to removing every word that is not necessary, every clause that is superfluous, and every sentence that does not carry its own weight. Every word, phrase, clause, and sentence must be in your memo for a purpose. That purpose must be to provide a clinical analysis of the issue presented by the facts before you.

Finally, while there are no special rules for the mechanics of a memo, there is something worth remembering. Whether you are a summer associate or a new associate in a law firm, your goal is to make a good impression on the partners. Most of you will probably buy new clothing to fit the firm's image. When you graduate, you will undoubtedly receive a new briefcase that fits the status of a new lawyer. Wouldn't it be a shame to destroy that carefully nurtured image by making grammatical mistakes in your memo? Do not depend on your secretary or typist. Nothing is less convincing than a lawyer (or law student) trying to cover up a mistake by saying "my secretary must have goofed." Take the time to proofread your memo. It is your work product and you should be proud of it in every way.

CONCLUSION

Remember to approach the task of writing a legal memorandum by following the essential steps that collectively make up the writing process. You will find that what started as a complex and dismaying task will become instead a logical sequence of smaller and more easily accomplished tasks.

SAMPLE MEMORANDA

Following are two sample memos. The first is an intraoffice memorandum, and the second is a memorandum of points and authorities.

Intraoffice Memorandum

The following memorandum was written by an Associate at a highly respected labor law firm.[1]

Date: October 8, 1992
To: Senior Partner
From: Associate
Re: Jane Smith—Indemnification Issues

ISSUES

The issue is whether indemnification provisions akin to those contained in Labor Code § 2802 exist for employees of public entities as well. Two aspects will be considered.

Issue Number 1. Is an employee of the Utopia School District entitled to indemnification for alleged discriminatory acts committed in her official capacity?

---

[1] Thanks to Alan Berkowitz for allowing us to use this memorandum.

Issue Number 2. Is the Utopia School District required to provide Smith with a defense?

SUMMARY OF CONCLUSION

Issue Number 1. Yes, Smith should be entitled to indemnification.

Issue Number 2. Yes, except with respect to the defense of an administrative proceeding.

FACTS

Our client, Jane Smith, is a senior manager in the Utopia School District. Allegations of disability discrimination have been made against the district, arising out of an employment decision in which Smith was involved. Although to date Smith has not been named as a defendant, she has asked us to advise her on her right to indemnification by the district should that occur.

DISCUSSION

Section 825 of the Government Code imposes upon a public entity in California the obligation to indemnify its employees and former employees for injuries occurring within the scope of that employee's employment. Specifically, the statute states:

> If an employee or former employee of a public entity requests the public entity to defend him against any claim or action against him for an injury arising out of an act or omission occurring within the scope of his employment as an employee of the public entity and such request is made in writing not less than 10 days before the day of trial . . . the public entity shall pay any judgment based thereon or any compromise or settlement of the claim or an action to which the public entity has agreed. (Gov't) Code § 825 (Deering, Supp. 1992).

Additionally, § 995 requires the public entity to provide a defense for its employees.

> [U]pon the request of an employee or former employee, the public entity shall provide for the defense of any civil action or proceeding brought

against him, in his official or individual capacity or both, on account of an act or omission in the scope of his employment as an employee of the public entity. Cal. [Gov't] Code § 995 (Deering 1982). The only limitations to this duty are that the public entity does not have to provide a defense if the public employee acted outside her scope of employment; she acted because of fraud, corruption or actual malice; or a conflict of interest would be created between the public employee and the public entity. Section 995.2. Assuming that none of these factors exist, Ms. Smith should be entitled to a defense to any civil suit brought against her and the Utopia School District would be obligated to pay any judgment taken against her.

It should be noted that the public entity is *not* required to provide for the defense of an *administrative* proceeding brought against an employee. Despite this, the public entity may do so if the act complained of occurred within the scope of employment and such a defense would be in the best interests of the public entity. Additionally, the employee must have acted in good faith, without actual malice, and in the apparent interest of the public entity. Cal. [Gov't] Code § 995.6 (Deering 1982).

During research, a question arose as to whether the indemnification provisions applied to actions based on discrimination. The above-cited provisions have typically been litigated in the context of tort claims brought against a public employee. A 1976 California Supreme Court case should dispel any notion that the indemnification provisions are so limited in scope. In *Williams v. Horvath,* 129 Cal. Rptr. 453 (Cal. 1976), the Supreme Court held that section 825 was not limited to those actions based in tort. The Court said:

> There is nothing whatever in the language of section 825 to suggest that governmental employees are to be indemnified only if the cause of action upon which liability was predicated had its source in the tort Claims Act. On the contrary, the specific reference in section 825 to *any* claim or action negates this inference. 129 Cal. Rptr. at 459 (Emphasis in original).

Thus, in *Williams,* police officers who allegedly violated federal statute 42 U.S.C.A. section 1983 by assaulting and battering the plaintiffs were entitled to statutory indemnification from the city with respect to any judgment that might be entered against them. The broad language from the Supreme Court's opinion quoted above, coupled with the fact that *Williams* involved a federal civil rights claim under section 1983, should provide the necessary assurance that the indemnification provisions contained in the Government Code would apply to an action brought under state discrimination statutes.

CONCLUSION

Ms. Smith is entitled to indemnification for any judgment rendered against her, assuming that her actions were within the scope of her employment. Further, the district will be required to provide a defense for her should she request them to do so. (This does not apply in an administrative proceeding).

Finally, there is a question as to whether Ms. Smith had a right to engage her own private counsel as she was concerned that the district would not be providing adequate counsel. The public entity is specifically authorized to satisfy its obligation to provide a defense to the public employee by paying the fees of a privately engaged attorney. Cal. [Gov't] Code § 996 (Deering 1982). But, if the district is willing to provide a "reasonable" defense, it is doubtful that the district could be forced to pay outside fees simply because the employee was not satisfied with the choice of counsel.

Memorandum of Points and Authorities

This is the Memorandum of Points and Authorities which accompanied a motion for "Judgment of the Pleadings," or "Summary Judgment," and "Sanctions."[2] The writer is asking the Court to throw out the plaintiff's lawsuit because plaintiff lost his first suit on exactly the same dispute, and this is the second time he is suing

[2] Thanks to Peter Nussbaum for allowing us to reproduce this Memorandum of Points and Authorities.

about the same thing. The principle of "res judicata" means that once you have lost a lawsuit you cannot give it another name and try suing again over the same dispute. "Sanctions" usually mean money. In this case the defendant says that the same lawyer who brought the first case, and knows all of the facts, brought the second case. She should be punished, defendant argues, because she is wasting the Court's time and forcing the defendant to spend its money defending against a frivolous lawsuit.

We have edited this memo for inclusion here. Following the title page (omitted here) is a table of contents.

Table of Contents

[We omit the Table of Authorities which follows, and go to the Introduction]

Introduction

The complaint in this action seeks damages against defendant, Alameda County Joint Apprenticeship and Training Committee for the Electrical Trade (JATC), for breach of contract and fraud based on defendant's alleged misconduct in administering a qualifying mathematics examination taken by plaintiff Gary Smith on May 21, 1988. . . . The essence of the complaint is that the results of plaintiff's mathematics examination were falsified by the JATC and that plaintiff has thereby been wrongfully denied advancement in the process to become an apprentice electrician.

Plaintiff's underlying claim is identical to one which he previously pursued, through the same attorney, against this very defendant in another action before this Court. . . . As disclosed by records of which this Court may take judicial notice, plaintiff in that earlier action sought damages against defendant for alleged discrimination, intentional infliction of emotional distress, and negligent infliction of emotional distress, *based on precisely the same alleged misconduct on which the current action is premised—falsification of test results and wrongful denial of advancement in the process to become an apprentice electrician.* After full consideration of the evidence and arguments of counsel in the prior case, the Court granted summary judgment in favor of defendants on March 20, 1990. The judgment in that action is final, no appeal having been taken.

That valid, final judgment is res judicata of the claims belatedly asserted by plaintiff in this action. Therefore, defendant moves for judgment on the pleadings on the ground that plaintiff has failed to state facts sufficient to constitute a claim upon which relief may be based. Moreover, in the interest of judicial economy, defendant also moves in the alternative for summary judgment on the ground that there exists no triable issue as to any material fact and defendant is entitled to judgment as a matter of law. . . .

Facts

The JATC has been approved by the State of California to train apprentice electricians to become journeypersons. On May 21, 1988, along with other applicants for the JATC program, plaintiff took a mathematics test designed as a preliminary screen to assess his basic math skills. . . . Each applicant, including plaintiff, was asked to print his or her name at the top of the answer sheet and sign it. Plaintiff did so, took the test, and scored 64 percent—below the minimum passing grade of 70 percent. . . . The JATC notified plaintiff on or about May 25, 1988, that he had failed. Because of his failure, plaintiff was eliminated as an applicant. . . .

[Several paragraphs describe the process of plaintiff contacting JATC and arranging to see the test booklet]

Eight months later, on August 7, 1989, plaintiff filed suit in this Court for damages against defendant alleging that the JATC had discriminated against him, based on his race, by purposely incorrectly scoring his mathematics test and thereby causing plaintiff to fail the examination and to be denied the opportunity to continue the process of applying for entrance into defendant's apprenticeship program. . . . Plaintiff claimed damages for lost income and emotional distress and also sought punitive damages. . . .

[A description of events leading up to the judgment is provided here.]

. . . on March 20, 1990, after a full hearing on the matter, Judge Hodge granted summary judgment in favor of defendant JATC. Plaintiff did not appeal from that final judgment.

On January 21, 1992, plaintiff, again represented by Ms. Kerl, filed a new complaint against the JATC seeking damages for alleged breach of contract and fraud based on plaintiff's claim that the JATC falsified his test results and forged his signature on the answer sheet. . . . When the complaint was brought to Mr. Nussbaum's attention [attorney for JATC], in the hope of avoiding wasteful litigation, he wrote to Ms. Kerl to inform her that the action was frivolous and barred under principles of res judicata. He also stated that if plaintiff did not dismiss his action the JATC would seek sanctions against both Mr. Smith and Ms. Kerl pursuant to CCP Section 128.5. . . . Mr. Nussbaum never heard from Ms. Kerl.

Argument

A. Defendant Is Entitled to Judgment on the Pleadings

A motion for judgment on the pleadings may be granted on the same ground on which a general demurrer is granted, i.e., that the complaint fails to state facts sufficient to constitute a claim under the appropriate substantive law. (*Colberg, Inc. v. California* (1971) 67 Cal.2d 408, 412.) Where the pleadings and matters judicially noticed establish a complete bar to an action, the complaint fails to allege facts sufficient to constitute a cause of action and judgment on the pleadings is appropriate. (*Dryden v. Tri-Valley Growers* (1977) 65 Cal.App.3d 990, 997–98.) Thus, if all of the facts necessary to show that an action is barred by res judicata are within the complaint or subject to judicial notice, the court may properly grant judgment on the pleadings. (*See Frommhagen v. Board of Supervisors* (1987) 197 Cal.App.3d 1292, 1299; *see also Carroll v. Puritan Leasing Co.* (1978) 77 Cal.App.3d 481, 486.)

[Other case citations and arguments follow on this point.]

B. *In The Alternative, Defendant Is Entitled to Summary Judgment*

A defendant may seek summary judgment in any case in which it is contended that "the action has no merit." . . . The motion "shall be granted if all the papers submitted show that there is no triable issue as to any material fact and that the moving party is entitled to judgment as a matter of law." (CCP §437c (c).)

If this Court does not grant defendant JATC's motion for judgment on the pleading, then defendant's motion for summary judgment should be granted in light of the evidence presented in support thereof. . . . That evidence demonstrates that plaintiff was aware of potential claims of breach of contract and fraud based on alleged forgery and had every opportunity in the prior action to advance those claims. Under the principles of res judicata discussed above, the final judgment in the first case adjudicated all issues that "might have been urged" by plaintiff. Pursuant to that judgment there are no triable issues as to any material fact regarding plaintiff's claims for breach of contract and fraud based on allegation of forgery and, therefore, defendant is entitled to judgment as a matter of law. . . .

[The argument and references continue for several more paragraphs.]

C. *Defendant Should Be Awarded Its Reasonable Expenses, Including Attorney's Fees*

CCP §128.5(a) provides that a court may order a party, *or its attorney,* or both, to pay "any reasonable expenses, including attorneys' fees, incurred by another party as a result of bad faith actions or tactics that are frivolous or solely intended to cause unnecessary delay." The phrase "actions or tactics" is defined to include the filing and service of a complaint (CCP §128.5(b) (1)); the term "frivolous" is defined as "totally and completely without merit." CCP §128.5 (b) (2). . . .

The courts have not hesitated to impose sanctions for the filing of a frivolous lawsuit (*see Finnie v. Town of Tiburon* (1988) 199 Cal.App.3d 1, 12; *Dwyer v. Crocker Nat'l Bank* (1987) 194 Cal.App.3d 1418); nor have they hesitated to award those sanctions against the attorney who filed the complaint. (*See Finnie v. Town of Tiburon*, supra.) Moreover, as the First Appellate District has held, it is not necessary to demonstrate that the party or attorney has willfully acted in bad faith. (*See On v. Cow Hollow Properties* (1990) 222 Cal.App.3d 1568, 1575–76; *see also Wertheimer v. Acret* (1992) 4 Cal.App.4th 100, 108 & n.9; *In re Marriage of Gumabao* (1984) 150 Cal.App.3d 572, 577.) The standard is an "objective" one. (*Finnie v. Town of Tiburon*, supra, 199 Cal. App.3d at 12.) Thus a motion has been held to be "frivolous" under CCP §128.5 where "any reasonable attorney would agree that such motion is totally devoid of merit." (*M.E. Gray Co. v. Gray* (1985) 163 Cal.App.3d 1025, 1034.) The same standard should apply to the filing of a lawsuit.

[Several more paragraphs of argument follow.]

Argument

For the reasons stated above, the Court should grant defendants' motion for judgment on the pleadings. In the alternative, the Court should grant defendants' motion for summary judgment. In either case, the Court should grant defendants' motion for attorney's fees pursuant to CCP §128.5.

Respectfully Submitted, . . .

CHAPTER FIVE
Writing Legal Briefs

INTRODUCTION

The third type of legal writing assignment common to law schools is the legal brief. In this chapter we will go through the writing process involved in preparing a persuasive legal brief.

A brief is a formal written document arguing your client's position. The brief is written for and submitted to a court. Unlike the office memo, it is an advocacy document. The goal in brief-writing is to convince the court of the correctness of your client's position. Your job as an advocate is to present the client's case as clearly, compellingly, and attractively as possible.

FORMAT

The format for briefs, unlike the memorandum, is strictly controlled. A brief must conform to the rules of the court in which it is to be presented. Because courts vary significantly, we have presented the rules for briefs contained in Rule 28 of the Federal Rules of Appellate Procedures. We have omitted data on technical format (such as typeface and type size) because these are not important for our purposes. We also omit reference to any variations of a particular circuit.

According to Rule 28 of the Federal Rules of Appellate Procedure, the appellant's brief contains five elements. The first element is a table of contents with page references and a table of cases that is alphabetically arranged and that refers to the page of the brief where each case is cited. The second is a statement of the issues presented; the third, a statement of the case; the fourth, an argument; and the fifth, a conclusion. Each of these elements will be discussed sequentially.

Table of Contents and Table of Cases

The requirement of a table of contents and a table of cases provides the first opportunity to begin arguing your case. On the surface this claim may sound improbable. After all, we are not accustomed to seeing argumentative tables of contents. There is, however, an important difference in the brief. That is, the table of contents not only contains the page references to where a specific section of the brief starts and the pages on which a particular case is cited, but also the pages on which each portion of your argument begins.

Your argument section will be broken down by "point headings." These point headings are argumentative statements of a portion of your overall argument. For instance, a point heading might read as follows: "Section 1234 of the Civil Code requires that the suit be brought within three years of the event. Because this suit was brought four years and three months after the event, plaintiff is barred by the statute from bringing this action." Your point headings in the table of contents should form a succinct legal syllogism that makes the case for your client. After reading only your table of contents, it should appear to the judge that there is a good reason for deciding the issue in your favor.

Statement of Issues

The second part of the brief is the statement of the issue or issues presented for review. The issue is normally presented in the form of a question. In writing your issue, the goal should be to frame the issue in such a way as to include the key facts of this specific case. The question, together with its implied answer, should succinctly state the holding that you want the court to reach. For example, you might write, "Will the court specifically enforce the agreement to make repairs necessitated by fire, according to the express provision of a lease between plaintiff-lessee and defendant lessor?" You should note that we did not put this in the more general form of, "Will the court enforce specific performance of a lease provision?" Rather, we included a specific fact from our case— that there was an agreement to repair fire damage—in order to make the issue fact specific. By making the issue fact specific, you avoid what might otherwise appear to be hypothetical questions, and you encourage the reader to answer the question in your favor.

Statement of the Case

The third element of the brief is a statement of the case. It contains two parts. First, according to Rule 28 (a) (3), "the statement shall first indicate briefly the nature of the case, the course of proceedings, and its disposition in the court below." The statement itself should tell the court the general nature of the action, the person who is taking the appeal, the court from whose determination the appeal is being taken, whether the appeal followed a trial by judge or judge and jury, and the disposition of the case by the court or courts below. For example, "This is an action, based on negligence and nuisance, to recover damages for injuries sustained by the plaintiff. Defendant appeals from a judgment of $5,119 entered upon a $5,000 verdict in favor of the plaintiff at a jury trial in Supreme Court King's County, and from an order of Justice Johnson denying the motion to set aside the verdict." As you can see, the statement of the case answers all of the questions we suggested initially.

In addition to the statement of how this case got before the appellate court, a statement of the case contains a statement of "the facts relevant to the issues presented for review, with appropriate references to the record." While the statement of facts is your first extended opportunity to argue the case, it should not appear to be argument. You are trying to present facts in the light most favorable to your case. One of the most common mistakes that students make is to simply present the facts in chronological order with adjectives added to embellish an otherwise dull description. To assure a sense of completeness, you may be tempted to throw in every minor fact that appears in the record. Avoid these temptations. While it is sometimes useful to use a chronological presentation, you must carefully select the key facts necessary for your legal argument and the minimum number of additional facts that will permit the reader to understand what happened.

It is often much better to violate strict chronological order and begin with a compelling fact. For example, "Plaintiff had his nose, jaw, and arm broken while attempting to board defendant's train at the 42nd Street terminal at 5:30 p.m. on March 10, 1986." As you read that first sentence, you are probably curious as to what caused these injuries and why defendant is responsible for them. That is precisely what the writer wants you to feel. Your curiosity will carry you through a great many additional facts, chronologically arranged.

Argument

The fourth element of the brief is the argument section. In United States Supreme Court cases, it is normally preceded by a "Summary of Argument" because the argument itself is likely to be lengthy. The argument, according to Rule 28 (a) (4), "shall contain the contentions of the Appellant with respect to the issues presented, and the reasons therefore, with citations to the authorities, statutes and parts of the records relied upon." While you must follow the requirement of this rule, you should avoid following its style. Rather, the argument should be as straightforward as possible. Your goal is not to write an abstract treatise on the law, but to convince the court that justice requires both the rule and result that you are contending for in this case.

The argument section itself is usually divided into points, each of which has a point heading. The point headings, as we previously indicated, provide succinct statements of your major and minor premises as well as your conclusions. In developing each point heading under your argument, you must establish the appropriate authority for your statement, tie it in with the facts found in the record below, and show how it leads to the conclusion you want the court to reach.

Conclusion

The fifth section of the brief is the conclusion. It must contain the specific relief you are requesting. It can be an opportunity to make your argument one last time. Unfortunately, many writers simply give up. They preface their request for relief with a statement such as, "For all the foregoing reasons. . . ." This statement requires the reader to remember all of the reasons argued in the brief. While that may not be a problem if the brief contains only a few pages of argument, if the brief is lengthy, the reader is unlikely to remember all of the arguments. In this section you can restate at least the major points in your argument so that you remind the reader of your most compelling arguments.

WRITING THE BRIEF

Pre-Writing

Purpose. There is only one purpose in writing a brief: to persuade the court to rule in your client's favor. The distinguishing feature of the brief is its persuasiveness. It is an advocacy document, not an abstract treatise. Everything must be directed toward gaining conviction in your reader. While it might be interesting to include brief forays into other areas of the law touched upon by your argument, you must avoid any tendency to wander. Anything that will distract the reader must be pruned from the brief. Anything that will lessen the reader's confidence in the writer's authority (particularly some of the errors we talk about under "Clarity and Style" as well as mechanics) must be avoided. In short, the brief is one of the most single-minded documents you will ever be asked to compose. Everything in it is tightly controlled by your persuasive purpose.

Audience. The audience for your brief is a court. While that statement is so obvious that it may seem foolish to include it, there are some consequences that flow from having this particular audience. First, every judge has been to law school. That means that the judge has acquired certain habits of mind that are taught in law school. Among these is the reverence for authority that we call "precedents." Judges also believe, to a greater or lesser extent, in *stare decisis*, the doctrine that principles of law established by judicial decision be accepted as authority in similar cases. Second, judges as a group can be counted on always to prefer logical arguments to those that are transparently emotional. Third, judges expect that you will back up what you say by citing legal authorities supporting each of the points in your argument. Fourth, judges are not likely to be impressed by the use of a bombastic style, legal Latinisms, legal doublings (such as "give and devise"), or sentences so complex and recondite that they rival the worst eighteenth-century legal prose.

It is tempting to overanalyze your audience in writing a brief. That is, practicing lawyers often have a "book" on local judges. They attempt to ascertain what the judge likes from previous decisions the judge has written. There is, of course, nothing wrong with this as a general practice. On the other hand, the novice can easily be misled by assertions about what old Judge So-and-So likes. Indeed, it would be a mistake simply to accept that sort of advice. Rather, you should use the general advice we have given in the previous paragraph unless or until you believe that you have some special insight into a particular judge, based on his or her written opinions.

Voice.   It is common for students to attempt to sound as if they walk hand in hand with the justices of the Supreme Court. Usually, in attempting this, they sound as if they were coached by Larsen E. Pettifogger, the caricature lawyer in the comic strip *The Wizard of Id.* In attempting formality, they wind up sounding pompous. In attempting to "elevate" the tone of a brief, they wind up writing impenetrable prose. In attempting to sound authoritative, they wind up using words that confuse the reader. Finally, in attempting to make a trivial point sound important, writers wind up sounding as if they have absolutely no judgment.

The most persuasive voice in a brief is one that gives the appearance of objectivity while relentlessly arguing the client's point of view. That is easy to say, but difficult to do. There are a few guidelines that may be helpful. First, if you characterize your own or your opponent's arguments, you do not look objective. You may, in fact, seem shrill. This characterization can take the form of simply adding adjectives. As we discuss under "Organizing," there are other ways to emphasize your point. Second, never misquote a case, take a quote out of context so as to change its meaning, or make the assertion that a case stands for a certain proposition when that is palpably untrue. Not only do these tactics violate ethical constraints, but once you have been found out at them, your credibility is destroyed. Third, do not demean your opponent's arguments; defeat them with your own. If one of your opponent's arguments is silly, it is better to show it than to say it. By doing the latter you give the appearance of being a guide in the court's "search for truth and justice" rather than a shrill merchant hawking his wares.

Analysis. In preparing to write the brief you will be reading cases, organizing them, making generalizations from their holdings, and making analogies that will be useful to your argument. In short, you will be exercising the analytical and reasoning skills of a lawyer. In this section, we want to focus on how to generalize from cases, how to make analogies, and how to format your legal arguments. We shall begin by examining what we call the "legal syllogism."

A syllogism, as you may have learned in college, is a series of statements that, if properly put together, lead to an inevitable conclusion. For instance: "All men are mortal. Socrates is a man. Therefore, Socrates is mortal." This is a categorical syllogism upon which millions of beginning rhetoric students have cut their teeth.

Many of you learned a series of rules for determining the validity of any syllogism. It is not our intention to recite them here. Rather, we need to look at what the logic of a syllogism implies. It implies three things. First, there is fixed general principle, which in logic is often called the major premise. In a legal syllogism this is the "rule of law." Second, there will be a fact that belongs intrinsically and obviously to a class of things to which the general principle applies. In logic this is called the minor premise. In a legal syllogism these are facts that are in the record. Third, there will be a conclusion that automatically follows from the conjunction of the major and minor premises.

If we look at a syllogism related to the law, we can see certain problems. For example, examine the following syllogism. "Possession of marijuana is an infraction. John possessed marijuana. John committed an infraction." While this syllogism is logically correct, it has some real-world flaws. First, the law rarely has perfect, fixed principles with which to operate. For instance, as you may know, certain toxicologists or researchers may possess marijuana if they are licensed by the appropriate government agency. As a result, our initial statement cannot be quite categorical and therefore cannot meet the requirements of a major premise in a categorical syllogism. The problem in law is to find statements of general principle and of particular facts that are worth using as premises because they bear some significant relationship to the real world.

The way you will create syllogisms and arguments in your brief is through a process that may, at first blush, appear almost improper. Lawyers begin with the conclusion that is favorable to their client. In preparing to write your brief, you too will begin by looking for a legal conclusion that is favorable to your client. Your second task, of course, is to analyze the available facts to construct a favorable statement of facts that can serve as a minor premise in the syllogism. Once you have done these two things, your most difficult task begins. You must search through the cases to find an existing rule, a rule that can be created through generalization or a rule that can be created by analogy to serve as a major premise. As we noted when discussing the research/analysis feedback loop, as you do research and your acquaintance with rules widens, you may have to alter your perspective. That is, you may select among the facts to put together those that will make a suitable minor premise. Alternatively, you may find that the facts need to be cast in a different light to come up with a suitable minor premise. If neither is possible, you may modify your choice of rules to select one that more closely fits your factual situation.

Ultimately, to argue to the court in your brief, you construct a legal syllogism that contains the following.

A. A rule of law that can be extracted from prior cases.
B. Facts from your case that clearly fit within the rule.
C. A conclusion that follows and is favorable to your client.

It is, of course, easy to state this as a principle and as a logical construct. The more difficult task is to find those rules that will serve as major premises. In addition to research, this requires that you go through two other processes: generalization and analogy. Much of the first year of law school is devoted to teaching students how to generalize from cases. That is, you first learn to extract a rule, which is usually called a "holding," from a case. You then learn how to take several holdings, put them together, and come up with a rule governing a broader class of situations.

There are three major tests that you must apply to the generalization to determine whether it is valid. First, you must investigate a fair number of instances. That is, you cannot rely on a single case in the area of law. (Of course, if there is only one case in the area of law, you must rely on it.) Rather, you must examine a representative sample of the cases in an area before you make your generalization.

Second, the instances you investigate must be typical. That is, you cannot rely on an aberrant decision from a peculiar lower court. Nor can you rely on one that turns on truly extraordinary facts. Neither will serve you well in generalization. Rather, you will find that after reading several cases, what is "typical" will become quite clear to you.

Third, all of the negative instances must be explained for your generalization to be correct. If you do this, you will "distinguish" cases that are atypical. These cases, which might otherwise disprove your hypothesis as to what the rule is, are often distinguished by showing the factual differences between them and your case. In other instances, it may be the reasoning of the case that is faulty and that enables you to distinguish it. By applying these three analytical tests, you will be able to reach proper generalizations that will serve as major premises for your legal syllogisms.

The other way you can arrive at a proper major premise is through analogy. The process generally depends on the facts more than the rule of law. That is, in creating an analogy, you are attempting to show that your case is so similar to another case that the same rule of law should be applied and the same result reached. There are two important principles in making analogies.

First, the key facts of both cases must be similar in all important respects. While it is easy to say that, it should be clear immediately that you will have to make judgments as to what the key facts are. Again, this is what students learn to do in law school. You learn that the key facts of a case are the ones on which the decision rests. They are vital to the holding in a case, and without them, the holding would not be the same.

The second major principle you must apply is that the differences in facts must be accounted for as unimportant. Put another way, you must show that the facts that are not similar are also not key. Thus, through the process of analogy, you are able to use the facts of your case to determine the proper rule to be used in your major premise.

One other consideration is vital in your analysis. Almost all of your arguments will be "appeals to authority." That is, you will be arguing that the court should do such-and-such because of either precedents or *stare decisis*. In using the appeal to authority, you must keep three things in mind.

First, the court you are citing in your argument must be an appropriate authority for the court to which you must argue. For instance, a Superior Court decision in California is not precedential for the California Supreme Court. The reasoning might be persuasive, but the holding itself does not bind the Supreme Court.

Second, you must be sure that what you cite as the holding of a case is exactly that. In other words, not everything that a court says in an opinion is holding. The holding of the case, which may be phrased narrowly or broadly, is the only part of the case that has value as precedent. Again, discerning the holding in a case is a skill learned in law school.

Third, and this is by far the most subtle consideration, you must sometimes look behind the holding of a case. That is, when you wish to distinguish what appears to be a holding against you, you may want to look at the cases that the court relied on in reaching its holding. Unless you are dealing with the United States Supreme Court, whose analyses of its own holdings are authoritative simply because it is the Supreme Court, you may find that you can narrow the apparent basis on which a court held against your position. By examining the cases on which the court relied, you may be able to extract from them a principle that is narrower than the holding is generally thought to be. If so, you will be able to undercut your opponent's appeal to that authority.

There is nothing more critical than the time you spend in analyzing the cases before writing your brief. Quite often, what are perceived as writing problems are really thinking problems that result from a faulty or incomplete analysis. If you follow the principles we have outlined here, you will be well on your way to the kind of analysis that will enable you to write a successful brief.

Organizing.   In organizing your brief, you should follow the same principles we described under memorandum writing. The problem resulting from failing to follow the research/analysis feedback loop is worsened when you organize a brief. You have so much more material to cover that it is absolutely critical that you organize as you go along.

As you organize, two things will become apparent: your arguments are related to one another, and they are of different strengths. A basic and fairly common principle in organizing the argument section of your brief is that your strongest argument should come first and your second strongest argument last. This way, the first and last impression you leave on the reader are favorable to you. In addition, you should organize so that your proleptical arguments are buried within the arguments for your case. You will not want to put all of your opponent's arguments in one place or deal with them at one time. To do so would give them undue emphasis. Rather, you want to organize so that each of your opponent's arguments is surrounded by far more forceful arguments of your own.

Outlining. The principles of outlining that we discussed in the chapter on memorandum writing are equally applicable to brief writing. It is even more important, however, to have a good outline in writing a brief because of the length of the document.

Writing/Drafting

You can expect to do multiple drafts of the brief. Your constant effort will be to eliminate anything that is extraneous to your argument, to clarify your arguments and proleptical arguments, and to devastate your opponent's arguments. Unlike the memo, the brief is not a balanced, clinical document. Rather, it is an advocacy document and its writing must reflect that. In every portion of the argument section, your argument must take up more space than that of your opponent. As you revise you must find ways to be sure that the emphasis is always on what you want to say, not on what your opponent might argue.

Clarity and Style. The greatest challenge in brief writing is to express a complex series of interrelated arguments simply. It is absolutely critical that you work from an outline so that, in broad terms, you know where you are going at all times. Moreover, even as you are doing your first draft, you should beware of using words if you are uncertain of their meaning. That is often your first clue that you do not know your argument very well. Go back and learn the meaning of the word or phrase and then be sure you grasp the argument it embodies.

The second clue that you might be confused is long quotations. If you find the length of each quotation greatly exceeds the material that explains it, you may not understand your argument. Go back and examine your outline. Does it show only a case citation? If so, you are relying solely on a quotation to carry your argument. It may not be enough.

One other aspect of long quotations is worth remembering. Research by psycholinguists shows that most people do not read long quotations. If you are relying on a series of long quotations to carry your argument, your reliance is probably misplaced. Ask yourself what will happen to your argument if the reader skips all of the long quotations. If you are unhappy with the answer, shorten the quotations by eliminating everything that is not vital as authority. If necessary, prune the quotation by using ellipsis, those three little dots that tell the reader something has been omitted. Finally, if you cannot shorten the quotation, consider paraphrasing it. While a paraphrase is not as convincing as an actual quotation, it does have one advantage over the long quotation it replaces: it will be read.

Many students who write otherwise acceptable prose have severe style problems when drafting a brief. It is an important document, so they believe their prose should mirror its importance. It is a weighty document, so they believe their prose should have gravity. It is a document that may "make law," so they believe they should write for the ages. Struggling under this perceived burden, they panic. Everything they learned about legal writing goes out of their heads, and they wind up imitating the worst written decisions they have read. We do not have a pill to cure the common brief. We can offer no one-sentence formula for avoiding legalese. All we can say is that you should reread the chapter on style before drafting your brief. It is so easy to slip into obscure and Byzantine prose and so difficult to extract yourself when you are revising that we can only caution you to fortify yourself before you begin.

There are three common assumptions—all wrong—about what constitutes good style in a brief. First, writers assume that complex ideas require big words. Wrong. If you understand an idea yourself, you should be able to explain it with simple words. Some ideas require you to use specific, multisyllabic terms, but they are required far less commonly than you may think.

Second, writers assume that complex ideas can be expressed only in complex sentences. Wrong. You can break your idea down into its component parts and then write clear, direct sentences. If the idea is qualified in a number of ways, you do not have to include all of the qualifiers in the sentence that states the idea. You can begin with the idea itself then follow with the qualifiers in their order of importance. This will also help avoid giving the qualifiers and the idea equal sentence weight.

Third, writers assume that complex ideas must be expressed in single, marathon paragraphs. Wrong. Even a complex idea can be broken down into smaller ideas, each of which can form its own paragraph. Faced with long paragraphs, readers' eyes glaze over. They develop a compulsion to skip the paragraph, possibly missing your best argument. Do not provide that opportunity.

In attempting to get a good idea of a successful style, you may want to search out someone who wrote a good brief so that you can use it as a model. There is nothing intrinsically wrong with that. It can be a terrible problem, however, if you attempt to slavishly copy the style of the author. Most instructors have seen otherwise competent papers badly damaged by a student's attempt to copy the style of an example distributed in class. Some aspects of style are highly individual. You are unlikely to copy them successfully from another writer. If you try, you may well ruin your own writing.

That brings us to our last point about style. It should not call attention to itself. If it does, it will detract from your argument.

Unity and Coherence.   As we noted in the memo chapter, there is no substitute for organizing beforehand. If you do not know how you are going to get your argument from point A to point B, it is unlikely that your reader will understand how you got there. If you do not know how your ideas relate to one another, it is unlikely that your reader will be able to figure it out. Thus, the mechanical aspects of unity and coherence are less important than the underlying analysis.

What is important is the use of graphics, signposts, and transitions. The easiest way to use graphics is to copy the format of your outline in the argument section of your brief. For instance, if there are three major points you are making, begin each of them with a bold Roman numeral at the left edge of the text. Underline and italicize the point heading so that it is clearly visible. The first subheading should begin with a capital A, and be indented a few spaces. The next subheading should be indented further. Use white space to set off your headings so that they are clearly visible. As the reader goes through the brief, he or she will always know whether the point is a new one or part of an earlier one.

Signposts provide the verbal equivalent of the graphic devices we have just discussed. They show, within and between paragraphs, where the reader is in your argument. We have covered signposts in other sections of this book, so it should be sufficient to say that their most critical use is in the complex arguments embodied in a brief.

Like signposts, transitions let the reader know the relationship between different ideas. They move the reader from one point to the next with a minimum of idea juggling. They too have been covered in another section of this book, so we will only reiterate their importance in a document as long as a brief.

Revising

Because the brief is a long document, you should first revise it in sections, then as a single document. Specifically, there are three stages of revising a brief. First, you should examine each subsection separately. Ask yourself each of the questions for revision we introduced you to in Chapter 1. In your argument section you should ask yourself these questions about every subsection of the argument. It is easy to gloss over defects if you wait until the very last minute to ask yourself these revision questions. Instead, you should ask them initially after drafting one section and before drafting the next section. You should also take this opportunity to look at each section with your opponent's eyes. Later on, you should ask the questions as you look at each subsection in turn. That way, you can be assured that any idea you want the reader to remember from an earlier section is close enough so that it will be remembered. If not, you can repeat it.

Second, you should examine the document as a whole for consistency. Be sure that all of the facts you relied on in your argument actually appear in your fact section. Be sure that the cases you cite are listed in your table of cases. Check that your outline logic has been consistent and correct throughout the entire argument section. Check your use of terms to be sure that you have not given an old idea a new name somewhere in the middle of your argument. Check the conclusion against the issue. The conclusion should state positively the answer to the legal question posed in the issue. It should also contain the major points you made in the argument section. Finally, check the tone and style of the entire document. Have you been consistent throughout? If you notice that in some places your tone switches from persuasive to professorial, it may be a clue that you have wandered from the persuasive purpose of your brief. If so, examine the section carefully to determine whether it needs to be revised or simply omitted.

Editing

The third step is to edit carefully by proofreading the entire brief both for mechanical errors and technical correctness. We have written at length about the problems of mechanical errors and how they undercut your authority. You can refer to those earlier discussions. What we have not discussed is the importance of technical correctness. Correct citation form is only a part of it. You must also check to be sure that the citation itself is correct. There are few things more annoying to a reader who has taken the trouble to look up a case than to find that it does not exist where you say it is. Not only is that annoying, but it leads the reader to question both your competence and your honesty. If, when the reader finally finds the case, it turns out that the case does not stand for the proposition for which you cite it, your credibility is seriously compromised.

As we noted earlier, court rules dictate matters of print size, margins, and spacing. All that we can say is that those rules must be followed. The other set of rules that must be followed is the *Blue Book* citation forms.

Remember, mechanical errors will lower your authority in the eyes of the reader of the brief. Given the formality of the brief, it is critical that you eliminate any mechanical errors before submitting.

CONCLUSION

Writing your first brief may appear to be an impossible task. Almost all first-year law students have had the overwhelming feeling that they knew neither how nor what to write. But if you break the process into a series of steps, as with the memo, you will find that you will know where you are going and how to get there. Following a thorough and logical procedure will help ensure a successful legal brief.

SAMPLE LEGAL BRIEF

Following is a successful and well-written brief in a U.S. Supreme Court case in which a company's policy of excluding women of child-bearing age from battery manufacturing jobs—allegedly to protect fetuses who could be damaged *in utero* by lead—was found to be sex-based discrimination.[1] You can read the Court's decision in *International Union, United Automobile Aerospace and Agricultural Implement Workers of America, UAW, et al., v. Johnson Controls, Inc.,* 111 S. Ct. 1196; 113 L. Ed. 2d 158; 59 U.S.L.W. 4209 (1992). We have edited the brief to reduce its length and technical complexity (omitting the title page, for example), while trying to retain its flavor. You should pay careful attention to the tight organization of the brief, and the constant use of signals and transitions to keep the reader aware of where he or she is in the argument, and where the argument is going.

QUESTIONS PRESENTED FOR REVIEW

1. Where an employer policy excluding all fertile women from certain jobs because of concerns for the health of any fetus that those women may conceive is challenged as unlawful gender discrimination violative of Title VII of the Civil Rights Act of 1964:

   a. does the plaintiff or the defendant bear the burden of proving that the employer's justification for excluding women from certain jobs meets Title VII standards?

   b. is that the justification judged under the explicit provisions of the statutory affirmative defense for bona fide occupational qualifications or is the employer entitled to assert an additional, broader "legitimate business justification" defense not explicitly stated in the statute?

   c. if only the statutory bona fide occupational qualification defense is available, does a fetal protection purpose come within the bounds of that defense?

2. Are scientific animal studies insufficient as a matter of law to demonstrate a significant risk to humans due to the exposure to a toxic substance?

[A list of Parties To The Proceeding comes before the table of contents.]

---

[1] Thanks to Marsha S. Berzon for allowing us to use this brief here.

TABLE OF CONTENTS

[Table of Authorities follows. After the Jurisdiction is given and the Statutory Provisions Involved, comes the Statement of the Case.]

STATEMENT OF THE CASE

A. The Facts

1. The Exclusion of Women from Battery Manufacturing Positions

Johnson Controls, Inc. ("the employer" or "the company") is a manufacturer of batteries. Occupational exposure to lead, the primary material used in the battery manufacturing process, entails a health risk to workers, including a health risk of harm to fetuses conceived by workers. Pet. App., 32a.

In 1977, Johnson Controls instituted its first official policy regarding the employment of women in lead-exposed jobs. That policy stated:

> [P]rotection of the health of the unborn child is the immediate and direct responsibility of the prospective parents. While the medical profession and the company can support them in the exercise of this responsibility, it cannot assume it for them without simultaneously infringing their rights as persons . . .

> Since not all women who can become pregnant wish to become mothers, . . . it would appear to be illegal discrimination to treat all who are capable of pregnancy as though they will become pregnant. [Jt. App. 140.]

Consistent with that view, the company recommended that women who expected to have children choose non-lead-exposed jobs. The company did not, however, provide any guaranteed transfer for women who wished to leave lead-exposed jobs in order to protect any children they might be planning to have, nor did the company protect the prior wage rate of any women who did transfer.

In 1978, the Occupational Health and Safety Administration (hereafter OSHA), acting pursuant to its statutory authority to "promulgate any . . . occupational . . . health standard" (29 U.S.C. § 655), announced its Final Standard for Occupational Exposure to Lead. 43 Fed. Reg. 52952 *et. seq.*; 29 C.F.R. § 1916.1025 (1987). When that standard was being considered, OSHA devoted particular attention to the question whether the possible effect on fetuses carried by pregnant workers justified excluding women entirely from at least certain lead-exposed positions. 43 Fed. Reg. 52960. "No topic was covered in greater depth or from more vantage points than the subject of women in the lead industry." *Id.* On the basis of its close study of the question, OSHA concluded that "there is no basis whatsoever for the claim that women of childbearing age should be excluded from the workplace in order to protect the fetus or the course of pregnancy." . . .

In 1982, Johnson Controls, despite its own earlier pronouncements and those of OSHA, announced a broad exclusion of women from lead-exposed jobs:

> It is [Johnson Controls'] policy that women who are pregnant or who are capable of bearing children will not be placed into jobs involving lead exposure or which could expose them to lead through the exercise of job bidding, bumping, transfer or promotion rights. [Pet. App. 9a (emphasis added); see Jt. App. 80–86]

Johnson Controls' policy applied to particular positions based upon whether a *single* individual in that position (not the mean or median individual) showed a blood lead level of more than 30 μg/dl once in the past year. Jt. App. 81, 123. [footnote omitted] Moreover, even though the company conducts individual blood testing as often as monthly on other employees (Jt. App. 124), the employer did *not* allow any women seeking to be hired or promoted into lead-exposed positions to demonstrate through individual blood monitoring an ability to keep her blood lead level below 30 μg/dl. See Jt. App. 88–89 (Beaudoin) (blood lead levels at the same work station can vary based on individual metabolism, good hygiene, and use of respirators). And, there is no explanation in the record as to why the ban extended beyond the jobs actually exposed to lead. Finally, the company banned *all* women who could not prove their infertility from lead-exposed jobs, regardless of their family status, age, sexual orientation, fertility of sexual partner, or expressed intent to bear children.

The sum of the matter is that, in practical terms, the company barred women capable of bearing children from *all* manufacturing jobs in its battery plants (except a few held by incumbent women), and from some nonmanufacturing jobs as well. Jt. App. 56, 115.

2. Harms Caused by Lead

[This section contains a discussion of effects of exposure to lead in both men and women at blood levels above and below 30 μg/dl.]

A. The Proceedings Below

This challenge to Johnson Controls' policy excluding fertile women from battery manufacturing jobs was filed by eight employees, certified as representatives of a class of similarly situated employees, and the union representing the employees, the International Union, UAW. Among the individual plaintiffs were Mary Craig, who elected to have herself sterilized in order to avoid loss of a desirable employment position (Jt. App. 35, 62); several female employees (one of whom, Elsie Nason, was fifty years old and divorced) who were transferred from lead-exposed positions, with loss in compensation (Jt. App. 31, 32, 33, 35, 59, 60–61); and Donald Penney, a male employee whose request for a leave of absence for the purpose of lowering his blood lead level because he intended to become a father, was denied (Jt. App. 36, 66–69).

After discovery, the company sought, and the District Court granted, summary judgment. That court held:

> Because of the fetuses possibility of unknown existence to the mother and the severe risk of harm that may occur if exposed to lead, the fetal protection policy is not facially discriminatory . . . [Jt. App. 17.]

The District Court therefore treated the explicitly gender-based policy in this case as if the employer had adopted a neutral policy with only a disparate *impact* upon women as a group, and, applying an "expanded . . . business necessity defense," refused to invalidate the discriminatory policy. Jt. App. 17–20. [footnote omitted]

On appeal, the Seventh Circuit, sitting *en banc*, affirmed by a 7–4 vote. First, the Court of Appeals majority agreed with the district court's basic disparate impact/ business necessity approach (Pet. App. 27a), but went further, placing on the *plaintiff*, not on the employer, the burden of persuasion on the two key evidentiary issues that purportedly justify departure from ordinary facial discrimination analysis—whether the danger to fetuses is substantial, and whether there is fetal danger only due to female exposure, or due to male exposure as well. Pet. App. 28a–32a.

Second, although the District Court had declined to reach the issue, the Court of Appeals decided that "Johnson Controls' fetal protection policy could be upheld [on summary judgment] under the bona fide occupational qualification defense." Pet. App. 42a. Where a business may present some danger to the health of a fetus carried by an employee, providing perfect protection for the fetus, said the Court of Appeals, is part of the "essence" of the business. Pet. App. 48a. Rather than remanding for consideration of the factual elements of the bfoq defense, the Court of Appeals majority went on to review on its own the summary judgment record, and held that the defense was established. Pet. App. 50a–54a.

The four dissenters wrote three dissenting opinions. All the dissenters were of the view that a case such as this one must be analyzed as a facial discrimination case, as to which the only pertinent defense is the bfoq defense provided by § 703(e), 42 U.S.C. §2000e-2(e). Pet. App. 60a, 62a–64a, 75a–81a. Judge Easterbrook, joined by Judge Flaum, further maintained that the proffered justification—the moral imperative of protecting fetal health from mistaken parental risk assessments—does not, as a matter of law, meet the statutory standard of equal treatment of employees "similar in their ability or inability to work," and is not a legally cognizable bfoq. Pet. App. 81a–87a. Judges Posner and Cudahy, in contrast, were of the view that the bfoq defense may, in very narrow circumstances, be available for justifying fetal protection policies, but believed that it was entirely inappropriate to grant summary judgment for the employer on the present record. Pet. App. 60a, 70a–74a.

SUMMARY OF ARGUMENT

I. By proving that Johnson Controls' fetal protection policy explicitly establishes an additional job qualification, proof of infertility, for all women and no men, the plaintiffs have met their burden under Title VII of demonstrating a violation of the proscription against making gender-based employment decisions. This conclusion does not change with the observation that only women can bear children. In enacting the Pregnancy Discrimination Act ("PDA") in 1978, Congress specifically intended to proscribe as gender-based discrimination distinctions based upon childbearing capacity, recognizing that such distinctions were the basis for many of the policies that had relegated women to inferior status in the workplace. Johnson Controls' policy also violates the three underlying purposes of proscribing explicit sex discrimination in the workplace: assuring the treatment of employees individually, rather than as members of proscribed groups; preventing gender-based stereotypes from tainting the decision-making process and stigmatizing women; and making certain that those policies that adversely affect women, even unavoidably, do not institutionalize their detrimental effect, but instead change in response to relevant background changes.

II. Under Title VII, an employer can justify facial sex discrimination in distributing employment opportunities only under the § 703 (e) exception for bona fide occupational qualifications ("bfoq"). That affirmative defense is an extremely limited one, and has no application here. First, both Title VII precedents and the PDA make clear that only requirements relating to effective job performance can constitute a bfoq. Absent this limitation, employers would be free to subordinate the basic nondiscrimination norm of Title VII to their individual values, rely upon non-job-performance related goals as a cover for discriminatory assumptions or stereotyped thinking, and decide complex health issues based on their needs rather than on the determinations made by agencies, such as the Occupational Safety and Health Administration, designated by Congress. Secondly, if available, a bfoq defense based upon fetal protection concerns would be far from narrow, and indeed could severely undermine the Title VII proscription upon sex discrimination in employment. Finally, to meet bfoq standards in the present situation, at the very least an employer would have to show that the fetal harms sought to be avoided are only mediated through women; that the company protects occupational health generally at the same level as it protects fetal health; that fetal concerns relate to the "essence" of the particular business on some basis *not* applicable to businesses generally; and that the *degree* of protection provided is "reasonably necessary" to the business. The Court of Appeals either made no inquiry into or committed error in considering each of these requirements.

ARGUMENT

In this case the petitioners challenge Johnson Controls' policy providing that "[a]ll women except those whose inability to bear children is medically documented" are barred from "jobs involving lead exposure or which could expose them to lead through the exercise of job bidding, bumping, transfer or promotion rights." Jt. App. 81, 85, 86. . . . It is our contention that this policy, on its face, constitutes disparate treatment of women in violation of § 703(a) of Title VII of the Civil Rights Act of 1964, as amended, 42 U.S.C. § 2000e *et seq.*; that the employer has not met its affirmative burden of demonstrating that the policy is saved by the "bona fide occupational qualification" defense stated in § 703(e) (the "bfoq" defense); and that Title VII does not provide any defense other than the bfoq defense for employer policies that constitute facial sex discrimination. We treat with § 703(a) in part I of our argument and with the affirmative defense aspect of this case in part II.

I. Johnson Controls' Fetal Protection Policy Constitutes Facial Discrimination on the Basis of Sex.

A. The two basic legal principles that govern a Title VII facial discrimination case such as this one and determine whether the plaintiffs have carried their initial burden of proof are now clearly established. . . . [argument and case references omitted]

B. (1) The employment policy at issue sorts eligible from ineligible employees by establishing different job qualifications and procedures along explicit gender lines: Women generally, *but no men*, are presumed ineligible for certain jobs, and are denied covered jobs unless they come forward with information regarding their reproductive capacity. . . . [argument and cases omitted]

(2) Viewing Johnson Controls' fetal protection policy more narrowly—and thus more favorably to the company— as one that excludes from covered positions the subgroup of women with the capacity to bear children, does not alter the conclusion that the policy on its face violates the Title VII proscription upon "us[ing] gender as a criterion in employment." *Price Waterhouse v. Hopkins*, 109 S. Ct. at 1789 (plurality opinion). . . . [argument and case references omitted]

C. Thus, whatever view one takes of the precise classification upon which Johnson Controls' fetal protection policy turns, that classification constitutes facial sex discrimination within the meaning of Title VII. And, Johnson Controls' policy violates not only the letter but each of the underlying purposes of Title VII's basic proscription of explicit gender-based distinctions. . . . [argument and case references omitted]

II. Johnson Controls' Fetal Protection Policy Cannot Be Justified as a Bona Fide Occupational Qualification within the Meaning of § 703(e) of Title VII. . . .

[Following this is a careful argument supported by case references leading to the conclusion that the judgment should be reversed. In fact, the brief was successful and the judgment was reversed.]

CHAPTER SIX
Logic and Argument

INTRODUCTION

"You can't argue with logic." At least that's what one of our friends is fond of saying. And we couldn't argue with her statement once we understood what she was saying. A "logical" argument is an extremely compelling argument. If we accept the premises of an argument, it becomes difficult to disagree with its conclusions. As mentioned earlier, the California Bar Examiners require that an applicant demonstrate an ability to "reason logically" in answering law questions. Indeed, if we were to attempt to identify the one characteristic that everyone agrees lawyers should have, it would probably be an ability to think logically. However, all of this agreement is encouraging without being enlightening. While we may agree on the importance of logic, it is much more difficult to define what we mean by logic.

Logic, as lawyers and law professors use that term, involves a kind of problem analysis that we call "linear," a kind of argument that we call "law structured," and the observation of certain conventions of rhetoric and language. These conventions require the avoidance of certain common "fallacies" of argument and the ability to recognize slanted language.

In this chapter we describe linear analysis to provide you with an approach that will help you analyze legal questions, whether they occur in an exam, memo, brief, or practice. We dissect and examine the law-structured argument, so that you can reproduce it when necessary or use it as a tool to discover the flaws in your opponent's arguments. We delineate the conventions that you must observe to avoid making your argument an easy target for your opponent. Finally—and this can be fun—we explore slanted language so that you can recognize it when it is used against you and skillfully employ it as you present your own arguments.

LINEAR ANALYSIS

While the term may seem a bit forbidding, all we mean by linear analysis is the taking apart of a law problem, dividing it into its constituent parts (e.g., torts or crimes), further subdividing those parts into their elements, and, finally, deciding whether each of those elements is present. The process is similar to what a computer programmer does when writing a program for a computer. Let us consider that analogy for a moment, because it may be instructive.

Computers, as you probably know, are basically a series of on/off switches. A computer "decision" is reached on the basis of many smaller decisions, each of which amounts to no more than yes/no, on/off. What is crucial for a programmer is to design a series of questions that can be answered yes or no so that a computer can "reason" its way through these questions to a final answer. While the concept may seem too mechanistic for the law (and we don't mean to suggest that computers could make legal decisions), an analogous method is useful for students who are faced with a complicated law question.

There is a need for linear analysis because complex fact situations often bring near-paralysis to many students. The question seems so difficult that they don't know where to start. Crucial questions occur in profusion, recollections of vital bits of law pop into mind, and all the while—especially in an examination—time is flying swiftly past. But if you will learn to think like a computer programmer and take problems a step at a time, even the most challenging law problem will resolve itself into a series of decisions that can be reasoned through with relative ease.

Consider the following example.

Werner was standing at a bus stop when Ken came up beside him. "I don't like your looks," Ken said. Werner ignored him. "So, you're trying to start a fight, are you?" Ken continued. Werner ignored him. Ken punched Werner in the nose and then calmly walked away. Werner now wants to know if he can sue Ken for battery.

Your first reaction is probably, "Of course he can sue for battery." But how did you reach that conclusion? If you are like most people, you reached that conclusion through a process we might call "informed intuition." Knowing the requirements for battery and having then read a fact situation in which it seems clear that Ken did something "wrong," you quickly put them together and arrived at the conclusion that a battery had occurred. You are right, of course, but your "right" answer doesn't provide a methodology for those times when "informed intuition" just doesn't seem to be working. Let us look at how a computer might be programmed to handle that same problem.

To program a computer to solve the problem of whether Ken committed a battery, we would first have to have a working definition of battery. The definition we have used consists of six elements. Battery is (1) an intentional, (2) harmful, or (3) offensive (4) touching of another that is (5) unconsented and (6) unprivileged. Having broken this definition down into six elements, we could then ask whether each element is present in the fact situation. For the purpose of this analysis, we will allow ourselves only two possible answers, yes and no. Either an element is present or it is not.

Now at first glance this might seem absolutely wrongheaded. After all, part of being a good lawyer is the ability to argue either side of a case. True enough. But notice that no matter how elegantly you argue, to continue your analysis and reach a resolution of the problem, you must ultimately decide whether an element is present. If you are unable to decide if the element is present, you must assume either that it is present or absent to complete your analysis. On a law examination, if you had time, you would also analyze the problem in light of the other assumption.

Look at our facts and our definition again. Element (1) is "intent"; was there an intentional act on Ken's part? We could represent this question and its potential consequences in the chart shown below.

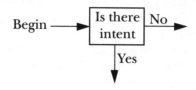

If we say that there was no intent on Ken's part (perhaps using the low-probability inference that he was the victim of a posthypnotic suggestion that rendered his will subject to someone else's control), we would arrive at the conclusion that there is no battery, because without intent there can be no battery. (In a law answer we would still consider the other possible elements conditionally, but for purposes of this illustration we will answer only yes or no.) If we answer yes, there was intent—and we probably will—then we must ask further questions, as illustrated in the chart on p. 109.

As you can see from the chart, sometimes the order in which we must ask the pertinent questions differs from the order in which we arrange an English sentence. Thus, before we can ask whether the touching was harmful or offensive, we must ask whether there *was* any touching. Notice that for the first two questions, if you answered no, you were forced to conclude that there had been no battery. However, our definition was worded disjunctively as to the nature of the touching. That is, there could be a battery if the touching was either harmful or offensive. Thus, if you found that there was a touching but that it was not harmful, you still would have to ask whether that touching was offensive, because that would be enough for there to be a battery.

Be careful, however, not to take yourself out of the problem. Most professors expect you to continue your discussion even if you believe that the answer to one of the questions might be no. Continue conditionally. "If there *were* intent . . ." You don't want to miss a chance to discuss an issue by concluding prematurely.

The charts we just examined dealt with only one tort, battery. However, in a model of your thinking for a law question you might well have a series of such flow charts, each dealing with a separate tort. Furthermore, the discrete flow charts might well be connected

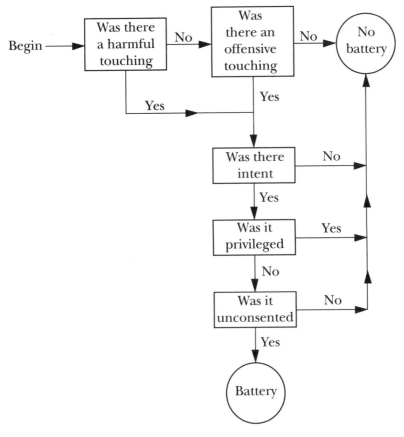

to one another by the logical relationships between the torts you are discussing. Remember that in discussing legal relationships in Chapter 2, we noted that sometimes the existence of one legal fact is a prerequisite for the existence of another. Thus, as we mentioned there, for someone to be liable as an accomplice, there must have been someone else who perpetrated the "target" crime. If we were creating a flow chart to "program" our way through a problem that potentially involved accomplice liability, we would have to note at each point where we reached a conclusion that the target offense had not been committed that there also could not be accomplice liability. It would only be at those points where we decided that the target offense had been committed that we could logically go on to discuss accomplice liability. Let us look again at the problem we discussed in Chapter 2.

Stan was a member of the Middletown Police Department, working as an undercover policeman. He was contacted by Ollie, who suggested that they hold up the neighborhood liquor store. Both men entered the liquor store together. Stan pointed a gun at the owner of the liquor store and handed him a note that read "I am a police officer. Hand me your money and pretend this is a robbery. I will return the money later." The owner did as he had been instructed and the two men left. Half an hour later Stan came back and returned the money. Was Ollie guilty of being an accomplice to a robbery?

To see how we would use linear analysis to work our way through this problem, we should establish some rules. First, let us say that an accomplice is someone who is (a) present at the scene of a crime and (b) aiding or (c) available to aid the perpetrator of the crime. Let us also define "robbery" as (a) the taking of (b) the property of another (c) through a threat of force (d) with the intent to deprive him or her of that property permanently. (These definitions are simplified for the purpose of illustration.)

As you can see from the definitions, there must be some crime that is occurring for an alleged accomplice to have been present at the scene of a crime. Let us see how our flow chart would look.

As you can see from the flow chart on p. 111, the question of whether Ollie could be guilty as an accomplice cannot be adequately analyzed until you have attempted to determine whether there was a robbery by Stan. While we will be talking about how to use qualifiers in your answers (and therefore take care of the problem of being unable to say *absolutely* whether an element was or was not present), you can see that this particular problem can be solved if you apply linear analysis.

By now you're probably getting a little skeptical. We have used fairly simple problems to illustrate our point, and you may wonder if the same analysis can work for complex problems. It can indeed. All you need to realize is that most complex problems are really just a series of finite, solvable, small problems intermeshed. Once you decide on the constituent torts, crimes, or other legal elements that must be considered, you can lay the problems out in your mind as we have done with our flow charts. We say "in your mind" because you probably have another objection.

When will you possibly have the time to prepare a flow chart as well as do everything else that we have suggested is necessary

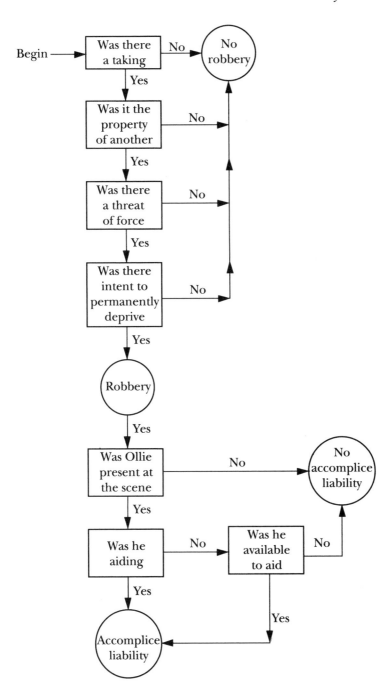

before you begin writing? You probably won't have the time in an exam. Remember that we are considering models for logic in this chapter. And this particular model can be extremely helpful in two situations. First, when you are not doing a timed writing exercise, it can help clarify your thinking before you begin outlining. When you have enough time, you can make up flow charts and experiment with alternative ways of analyzing a problem. Second, before you are required to write any answers, in or out of class, you can use this model to dissect the various theories of law you are learning about. It will help you to discover what a plaintiff would have to prove in a particular case, or what a defendant could use to defeat a plaintiff's case. It will focus your attention on the constituent elements of the law while allowing you to see how each element relates to those that come before or after it. If you practice analyzing legal problems with this model in mind, you will no longer have to rely on "informed intuition." You will be well on your way to thinking like a lawyer.

LAW-STRUCTURED ARGUMENTS

We have said it before, but it bears repeating. It's not the conclusion you reach that is vital, but how you got there. In law there are very few "right" answers. There are always uncertainties, contingencies, and unforeseeable consequences in any decision. That's why even the United States Supreme Court sometimes overrules an earlier decision. It is not that the earlier decision was reasoned incorrectly or even that new facts have come to light. It may simply be that times, and the composition of the Court, have changed.

If even the United States Supreme Court cannot always reach the elusive "right" decision, you shouldn't spend too much time worrying about whether you reached the right conclusion in a law problem. What you should worry about is how you reached your conclusion. To illustrate a model for a legal argument, let us construct a model by going through the process one step at a time.

First, we must attempt to identify exactly what we are doing in a legal argument. At the most basic level we are tying facts of legal significance to a legal conclusion. For example, "Penny punched Fran in the nose; therefore, she is liable for battery." The missing link in this argument should be fairly obvious. It is the legal theory known as battery. We could indicate this simple argument as follows.

Legal Theory

Fact ──────────────▶ Conclusion

In our representation it is the legal theory that connects fact and conclusion.

Often, however, it is not enough to state a legal theory and draw conclusions from it. In formal legal arguments, such as briefs and appellate decisions, the writer is required to "prove" that this is the "true" legal theory. The way in which this is done is by citing an authority (supplying a reference) that says this is the rule.

Ordinarily, when writing law examination answers, students are not required to remember all of the authorities that support their legal theory. However, to create a model that truly represents legal argument, we must include "authority" in our diagram. It would then look like this.

Legal Theory

Facts ──────────────▶ Conclusion

Authority

What this diagram indicates is that supporting every legal theory is an authority or set of authorities that could be cited to demonstrate that the legal theory is valid.

If your legal theory were battery, you might quote a definition of battery from the highest court of the state in which you were practicing. Consider the following example.

> The issue here is whether Arlene committed a battery on Randy. Battery, according to the Supreme Court of California, is the "intentional harmful or offensive touching of another." According to the facts, Arlene deliberately punched Randy in the jaw because he disagreed with her about whether the Yankees would win the pennant. . . .

As you have probably noticed, the definition of battery that we have used in this example is slightly different from the one we have been using all along. We have mentioned only what we earlier called the *"prima facie"* case. We have not mentioned what we might call the defenses.

Defenses are the elements of a tort, that, if present, defeat liability. That is, if Randy had consented to the punch in the jaw, or if—for some reason—Arlene was privileged to punch him, she would not be liable for battery. We can now indicate the position of defenses in our diagram.

Legal Theory

Facts ——————————▶ (Defenses) ——▶ Conclusion

Authority

What the diagram indicates is that you must consider the facts and the legal theory before you consider possible defenses. The defenses are interposed before the conclusion because they will significantly affect the conclusion you reach. That is, if you decide that a particular defense is present, you will be compelled to conclude that the particular tort did not occur.

There is only one more element that is necessary to complete our model of a legal argument, but it is the most difficult. To this point we have been constructing a model as if all of the conclusions you reach in a legal argument were absolute. Unfortunately, that is rarely the case. The facts almost inevitably show a maddening tendency not to fit into neat legal categories. Rather, you must usually reason by analogy, and analogies, by definition, are never perfect.

Analogies are, however, a vital mode of arguing in a legal context. This is so because the facts of a particular situation are almost never exactly the same as those that gave rise to a particular legal rule. Consequently, you must argue by analogy. In so doing you argue that the similarities between the fact situation in your case and the fact situation in the case that gave rise to the rule are so great that the rule of the prior case should control the disposition of your case. Analogies work when the significant facts in the two situations are similar and only the insignificant facts are dissimilar.

Whether a fact is significant, in turn, depends on your purpose in looking at the two situations. For example, let us say you were trying to argue that your case should be decided on the basis of a rule saying that manufacturers of autos must pay for any harm caused by the defective parts that they put in cars. It would be misguided to argue that the plaintiff in the case that established the rule and your plaintiff were both veterans of World War II. Nor would it be wise to argue that both cars involved were chartreuse. It might, however, be vital to show that both cars were brand new (which suggests that the defect was a manufacturing one) and that both were being used properly (which suggests that a part was truly defective and not just prey to intolerable abuse).

Of course the person who is arguing that the rule should apply will find that the facts that are similar are the significant ones, while the opponent will find that those same facts are less important. Be that as it may, we can say that analogies work when the crucial facts are similar and work less well the fewer crucial facts are similar.

Now, what does all of this have to do with uncertainty? In a legal argument you will frequently be forced to argue on the basis of an imperfect analogy. The facts will not be exactly the same on every significant point. Consequently, you will be forced to make a probability statement rather than an absolute statement. This, in turn, will make your conclusion conditional.

Let us consider a fact situation so that we can identify the elements that fit the categories of a model legal argument.

Owen has spent many years constructing the perfect kite. Wallace, who is an avid kite fighter, has a number of kites with ground glass glued onto their strings and with razor blades attached to their tails. On the day that Owen was test flying his perfect kite in Seafront Park, Wallace decided to attack. Wallace adroitly maneuvered his kite, causing the razor blades on the tail to cut the string on Owen's kite. As a result, the kite fell into the ocean. Infuriated, Owen decided to sue for battery. What result?

Now examine this analysis.

The issue is whether Owen has a cause of action in battery. According to the state Supreme Court, battery is the intentional harmful or offensive touching of another. Furthermore, the state Supreme Court has said that touching anything "intimately associated with another" is the same as touching that other.

Here it is clear from the facts that Wallace intended to cut the kite string, since he "adroitly maneuvered his kite, causing the razor blades" to cut Owen's string. That the touching was offensive to Owen is clear from the fact that he began this lawsuit. However, it is not clear whether cutting the kite string is "touching of another." *If the indirect touching of Owen through cutting his kite string is considered a touching of Owen himself* there would be a battery. While Wallace might argue that Owen had consented to having his string cut by flying his kite in Seafront Park, this defense should fail, because one does not ordinarily expect to have his kite string cut when flying a kite in a public park. Thus, Wallace might well be liable to Owen for battery.

Notice the following elements in this analysis. First, you can see that the writer has used the facts that were given. Second, you can see that the legal theory was articulated briefly and that the authority for it (the state Supreme Court) was mentioned. In applying the facts to the legal theory, the writer was unsure whether touching the kite string of another is the same as touching that other person. (Frankly, we could not be certain about how a court would rule on such an esoteric point.) Consequently, the writer made an uncertainty statement (italicized in our example) about whether cutting the string on a kite would be interpreted as the touching of another. Then the writer considered the possible defenses that Wallace could raise, and finished with a conclusion that was qualified by the uncertainty statement. If the writer had had time to be completely safe, a further conclusion, based on the opposite analysis from that embodied in the uncertainty statement in our example, could have been stated.

Here, with the uncertainty statement added, is a more complete model of what a legal argument looks like.

Legal Theory
Facts ——➤ (Uncertainty Statement)(Defenses) ——➤ Conclusion
Authority

This then, is the model of a law-structured argument. Facts are connected to a conclusion through a legal theory. The legal theory is backed up by an unquestionable authority. Before a conclusion is reached, the uncertainties of the fact situation are made explicit, and the defenses are raised and considered. Finally, a conclusion is reached, properly qualified by any uncertainty in the fact situation.

If you keep this model for legal argument in mind, you should be able to construct your own arguments with no difficulty. Again, you must remember that we are not trying in this chapter to give absolute, comprehensive rules for an immutable format. Rather, we are attempting to give you a model that you can use for patterning your own thought processes when you write an answer to a law question, a legal argument, or a brief.

FALLACIES OF ARGUMENT

Sometimes, as students work to analyze an issue, being careful to consider all aspects of the problem, they rely on fallacies of argument instead of focusing on the issue in question. While most law students quickly learn to avoid these fallacies, a brief examination should help to prevent writers from using fallacies instead of logic in their writing.

Appeal to Pity

Failing to find a reasonable defense to robbery in a law exam, one student referred to the defendant as a "loving father of six." That tribute to the defendant was not enough, however, to substitute for a reasoned evaluation of possible defenses.

Argument *ad Hominem*

The term *ad hominem* means literally "to the man." It describes an argument that is intended to disparage an opponent rather than address a matter at issue. Students sometimes characterize a person in a hypothetical problem in a most pejorative way to bolster a criminal charge or a conclusion of tort liability instead of emphasizing the logical argument leading to a reasonable conclusion. Here is a student example.

"The foul-mouthed bully is therefore liable for battery."

The characterization does not advance the argument. Remember always to emphasize the logic of a conclusion, for it is your analysis that scores the points.

Appeal to the People

This emotional argument is characterized by an attempt to rely on feelings of patriotism, justice, or common interest. One student offered a conclusion by declaring, "In the best interests of justice, the defendant should be convicted." Unfortunately, the legal basis for finding the defendant guilty was missing from the discussion.

The *Post Hoc* Fallacy

The full name of the *post hoc* fallacy is *"post hoc ergo propter hoc,"* which means literally "after this, therefore because of this." As you can see from the translation, the fallacy involves attributing causation to time sequence. It is easiest to spot when someone is using it to reinforce his or her own peculiar superstitious beliefs. For instance, many people say "It never fails. Every time I wash my car it rains." If people really believed that *because* they washed the car, *therefore* it rained, they would have been taken in by the *post hoc* fallacy.

Law students often run into difficulty with the *post hoc* fallacy when they assume that an event is caused by something that merely occurred before it in time. For instance, you might be told that, "Peter threw a firecracker at Mrs. Smith, who was in the seventh month of pregnancy. She was frightened by the explosion. The next day she had a miscarriage." Perhaps you would be tempted to conclude that Peter was the cause of Mrs. Smith's miscarriage. However, you could not reach that conclusion from these bare facts. While it is certainly a possible explanation of the miscarriage, it is not the only explanation. We don't know if this explosion *did* cause the miscarriage. Many other events could have intervened between the time of the explosion and the time of the miscarriage. If you already have it in your mind that the explosion caused the miscarriage, you might overlook another explanation that could occur later in the facts. Only when you have all the facts that are available to you should you make inferences.

Appeal to Authority

Finally, in legal writing the fallacy known as the "appeal to authority" often causes problems. It is often necessary to have an authority to cite to validate your legal theory. However, it is easy to misuse authorities, because what one court has said does not necessarily bind another court. You must be aware of whether the court to which you are writing (or hypothetical court in the case of a law exam) is bound by that other court's decisions. So, too, with statutes. They must be in force, and they must specifically cover the fact situation you are dealing with.

The difficulty comes in when using what lawyers call "dictum" as authority for a legal theory. The easiest way to explain dictum is through an analogy. If, when asked by your neighbor why you purchased your Brand X automobile, you reply that it was because your physician said it was the best automobile made, your purchase may have been made on the basis of the logical fallacy of an appeal to authority. You have accepted as authoritative someone's statement on a subject outside his or her area of expertise.

A judge's dictum is similar to the physician's statement on cars. It is nothing more or less than an opinion of a judge and was not integral to the judge's decision. The actual decision in the case is called the "holding," and only that can be authority for a legal theory. However, anything that was not essential to reaching that decision cannot be used as authority. Writers get into difficulty by quoting, as authority, statements that are merely dicta. In a case involving an alleged battery, the judge might have some observations about negligence. These observations would be dicta. If you were to quote this dicta on negligence in your answer to a negligence question, you would be using a fallacious appeal to authority.

SLANTED LANGUAGE

Because the authors of this text are both concerned with language (among other things), you might expect that we would use this opportunity to decry the vicious and abusive way in which some writers slant language to make their point. But we won't. In fact, we rather enjoy finding a piece of writing that is so cleverly slanted that we have a difficult time identifying the precise reasons that it is misleading. What we do want to warn against is an uncritical belief that words have one "meaning" that can be found in the dictionary. Words have a multiplicity of meanings, and a sophisticated user of the language can distinguish among the various shades and colorations of words. Our intention in this section is to make you more aware of *connotation, selection,* and *equivocation.* With practice you can learn both to recognize their place in slanting language and to use them effectively yourself.

Connotation

As English teachers use the word, "connotation" signifies that there are shades of meaning that distinguish words with similar meanings. Would you rather go out in a "boat" or a "yacht"? In the former you might drink beer and go barefoot; in the latter you might expect champagne and be prepared to dress in yachting attire. Both terms might refer to the same vessel, but there are distinct connotations involved in each term.

In legal writing the sophisticated use of connotation is absolutely vital. The attorney for the plaintiff in a battery case would be likely to say that his client was "hit" or "punched" by the defendant. The defendant's attorney would prefer to say that his client "touched" or "rebuffed" the plaintiff. In another case, dealing with whether an employee could be fired for not complying with a clause in the contract requiring union membership, the lawyer for the union said that the employee had "quit" the union; the employee claimed to have "resigned from the position."

Notice the difference between the use of connotation and the less sophisticated use of pejoratives. A different lawyer might have said that the defendant "viciously attacked" the plaintiff or that the employee, "with an utter disregard for the contract, quit the union." In both of these examples we have added explicitly pejorative words or phrases. In the first instance, the defendant's lawyer wouldn't even have to argue that "vicious" was a characterization added by the plaintiff—it stands out as an emotional flag being waved in the face of the reader. In the second instance, to cloud the issue, a clever opponent might show that the employee carefully took the contract into consideration in arriving at the decision to leave the union. In both cases, the explicit use of pejoratives can easily work against the writer.

When a writer merely uses a word that has a connotation favorable to the writer's point of view, the opponent has a much more difficult task. It would be awfully hard to argue that "quit" does not describe about the same thing as "resigned." But the effect of those two words on the reader is quite different.

Selection

When talking about slanted language, we use the term "selection" to indicate that a writer can color a reader's view of a particular event by the facts that are chosen. It is almost always true that when we are dealing with events in the real world, we cannot report every fact related to the event. For instance, if we were reporting on the content of a politician's speech at a Fourth of July picnic, we would be unlikely to mention that a member of the audience was wearing a gingham dress and sandals. However, if we were writing for the fashion page of a newspaper, we might find that an interesting fact to include. As you can see, our purpose in writing and our audience provide a principle for selecting which facts we are going to report.

This becomes particularly important in legal writing, because a good advocate can begin making an argument by carefully choosing which facts to report and which to omit. Consider the following event.

Algernon walked into St. Christopher's Church and removed all of the money from the poor box. A priest saw him take the money and called to him to put it back. Algernon became frightened and started to run home. The priest began to chase him. As Algernon was running across a busy street he knocked over a blind man. He tripped on the blind man's cane and stumbled into a woman. He pushed the woman out of his way and into the path of an oncoming car. The car struck the woman, causing her serious injury. She sues Algernon.

Let us consider an exaggerated version of the way you might present these facts if you were defending Algernon.

The defendant, on his way home from church, was tripped by a cane and stumbled into the plaintiff, pushing her into the path of an oncoming car.

Now look at the way you might present the facts if you were the lawyer for the injured woman.

The defendant, who had just robbed a church, was running across the street to escape pursuit. He first knocked over a blind man and then pushed the victim into the path of an oncoming car, causing her serious injury.

In both instances, we have selected those facts that are most favorable to the person we are representing. Though our example was exaggerated for effect, and we are not advocating such blatant manipulation of the language, we have not changed any facts nor have we used words with heavily prejudicial connotations. As you probably noticed, however, when representing the injured woman, we said "robbed the church" rather than describing exactly what took place, and we called the injured woman "the victim," thereby connoting her relationship with Algernon. The major effect, however, comes simply from selecting which facts to present and which to omit.

Equivocation

When a writer uses words or phrases that are deliberately ambiguous in the hope that they will be misinterpreted to the writer's advantage, he or she is using equivocation. The usual hope is that the writer can later insist on the "hidden" meaning and thereby gain some advantage. For instance, an unscrupulous used-car dealer might stress to a buyer that a particular car has been "reconditioned." The buyer might well interpret this to mean that the car has had all of its mechanical parts checked and replaced if needed, while the dealer might mean nothing more than that the car has been washed, polished, and vacuum cleaned.

Many people who have a low opinion of the law base their opinion on a belief that the law rewards equivocation. And, as a matter of fact, there is some justification for this belief. At one time, most courts followed a theory called the "objective" theory of contracts. According to this theory (we are oversimplifying it for the sake of illustration), words had only a single meaning. Both parties to the contract were presumed to know *that* single meaning of the words and to have intended to be bound by that meaning in their contract. This theory worked tolerably well when both sides were represented by astute counsel. However, when one party was represented by counsel and the other was not, the former had a great advantage. A lawyer could research each of the vital words that were used in the contract and learn what courts had said was the "meaning" of those words. The other party was then stuck with words whose "meaning" was not absolutely clear to him or her.

Courts have moved away from the "objective" theory, and many have adopted a rule for interpreting contracts that is more favorable to the lay person. That is, when the words in a contract are deemed ambiguous, they are interpreted against the person who wrote the contract. If that doesn't seem clear, perhaps an analogy will help.

Suppose that you have one piece of chocolate cake left and both your niece and nephew want it. If you want the division to be as fair as possible, you could tell your niece that she can divide the cake and your nephew that he can choose whichever piece he wants. The division is likely to be quite precise. The same principle is now at work in interpreting contracts. Thus, if the party drawing up a contract uses ambiguous language, he or she will not benefit by any equivocation.

CONCLUSION

Just as we hope that you will avoid equivocation, we hope that you will recognize and avoid the logical fallacies we talked about earlier. They are the negative parts of this chapter. The positive parts—connotation and selection in slanted language, linear analysis, and law-structured arguments—all require some practice to be useful to you. As you write answers for the law questions provided in the Appendix, practice making flow charts, and check your answers against the model for legal argument. In so doing, you will solidify your knowledge of the basic tools of logic lawyers use.

EXERCISE IN LANGUAGE

John Bent was shopping at the BOFFO store in Weehawken. After making a few purchases, he attempted to leave the store through the door he had used to enter the store. As he was walking toward the door a woman shouted, "I'm sorry, sir, but you cannot go out that way." John continued toward the door, ignoring the woman.

As he came within a few feet of the door, the assistant manager of the store darted in front of him, obstructing the door. Extending his arms so that they blocked the door, the assistant manager stood steadfastly in John's way. "You heard the woman," he said. "You must go out the regular exit." John attempted to walk past the assistant manager but was rebuffed by being pushed away from the door.

When the assistant manager pushed him away, John became angry. "Damn it," he shouted, "I have a right to go out any door I like!"

Calmly, the assistant manager replied, "Sorry, but you will have to go out the door marked 'Exit' that is down the aisle to your left." At this John began to yell and kick up a fuss about deprivation of his liberty. The assistant manager called over a store guard, who took John by the arm and led him to the exit. Just so that John would remember he was no longer welcome at BOFFO, the guard gave him a light kick in the seat of the pants as he unceremoniously escorted him through the exit.

You are counsel for John Bent, who has told you the foregoing information. Restate the following facts in the light most favorable to your client. You may use all of the information you have been given above.

1. As Bent was walking out the door, a woman shouted, "I'm sorry, sir, but you can't go out that way."
2. John ignored the woman.
3. The assistant manager of the store darted in front of him, blocking the door.
4. He extended his arms.
5. He stood steadfastly in John's way.
6. John was rebuffed when he attempted to go out the door.
7. The assistant manager called a store guard.
8. The guard took John by the arm and led him to the exit.
9. The guard kicked John lightly in the seat of the pants.
10. The guard led him through the exit.

CHAPTER SEVEN
The Mechanics
of Legal Writing

INTRODUCTION

More than a few students are certain that if only they hadn't drifted off somewhere back in the third grade or wherever and whenever grammar is taught—if they had not nonchalantly declined to acquire that esoteric grammatical knowledge in favor of mastering the infinitely more useful secret of the curveball—they would by now undoubtedly know how to write, and how to write beautifully and powerfully. It can only be the mysteries of the participle, or the gerund, or the split infinitive that, had they not been overlooked at that one cavalier time in life, would have revealed the secrets of composition.

Unfortunately, that is not quite true. No matter how much skill you have in diagraming sentences and identifying transitive and intransitive verbs, you still have to proceed beyond the sentence or paragraph level to become a good writer. There are, however, some writing faults at the paragraph and sentence levels that can cloud the meaning of your ideas and raise the eyebrows of your reader. While an awareness of the mechanics of sentence and paragraph construction will not assure smooth and persuasive writing, any breakdown in those mechanics can flaw an otherwise strong paper.

To increase your awareness of the mechanical elements of writing, to alert you to some very common writing faults that can confuse the reader, and to allay any nagging doubts about your own grammatical competence, we provide this chapter on the basic elements—the paragraphs and sentences—of persuasive writing.

THE STRUCTURE OF THE PARAGRAPH

"A paragraph is a number of sentences dealing with one central idea."

While this is a definition that teachers sometimes use, it doesn't take long to decide that it isn't very useful, especially considering the various sizes ideas come in. Some ideas, it is true, may be of the right size for a paragraph, but others are much larger—or even smaller.

While a history of the United States might occupy a substantial volume, a single portion of that subject, an intellectual history of the United States in the twentieth century, might require the same size volume. And a portion of that, a history of the United States foreign policy in World War II, could require just as many pages. The size of the volume would depend on the depth of coverage as well as the complexity of the idea. The same is true of the paragraph. Probably all of us remember high school papers in which equally complex subjects—"Youth's Major Problems," "The Future of the World," "My Life Goals"—were confidently dispensed within a single glorious paragraph.

In legal writing, especially in writing answers to law questions, the convention is to write short paragraphs. Each paragraph advances the argument or logical discussion one step at a time, and each subissue or element or legal problem requires a separate and short paragraph.

Topic Sentences

A topic sentence summarizes the contents of a single paragraph. In an essay, as distinguished from an answer to a law examination, legal memorandum, or brief, a thesis sentence would summarize the entire paper. In a law examination answer, however, because it consists of a number of separate discussions of separate issues, a thesis sentence referring to the entire answer is not necessary. Instead, think about separate topic sentences for each issue or subissue.

> Topic Sentence: The driver of the automobile may have a cause of action against the city for its failure to repair the street.
>
> Topic Sentence: The driver of the automobile may have a cause of action against the automobile manufacturer for the defect in the axle.
>
> Topic Sentence: The passenger may have a cause of action against the driver for his failure to obey the speed limit.

The topic sentence is used to focus the paragraph. Just as a coherent paper can be summarized by one thesis sentence, a coherent paragraph can be summarized by one even more specific sentence. If the paragraph cannot be summarized by one sentence, something is wrong: either there are too many ideas in the paragraph, or there is something extraneous in it that keeps it from being cohesive.

> Topic: In this situation, D, the driver of the automobile, may bring an action *against the city* for its negligent upkeep of the streets, and *against the automobile manufacturer* for the defectively produced axle. Since . . .

There are two issues indicated in this single paragraph: a suit against the city and a suit against the automobile manufacturer. A student who uses this topic sentence invites confusion, because the particular rules of law and the pertinent facts are different in each issue. You have to separate the issues and support each conclusion separately.

It is often helpful to consider a topic sentence before beginning to write a paragraph. Remember that your topic sentence should contain a single idea that you will develop through the use of specific facts.

Topic Sentence Placement

The next question is where to put the topic sentence in a paragraph. Consider this paragraph from a judicial opinion concerning the intentional infliction of mental distress.

> *The law cannot be expected to provide a civil remedy for every personal conflict in this crowded world.* Physical injuries to the person, inflicted either intentionally or through negligence, are actionable under familiar principles. Acts causing mental distress are in a different category. Oral or written statements which are false and defamatory, and which upon publication tend to deprive the victim of his good name, may be remedied in actions for libel and slander, although the orbit of the remedy has been narrowed within recent years. [Citations omitted.] On the other hand, offenses of a minor nature, such as name calling or angry looks, are not actionable though they may wound the feelings of the victim and cause some degree of emotional upset. This is because the law has no cure for trifles.[1]

In this paragraph, the first sentence is the topic sentence. It establishes what the paragraph will cover and explain. The last sentence, "This is because the law has no cure for trifles," refers only to "offenses of a minor nature" and not to all of the offenses in the paragraph, so it does not qualify as a topic sentence.

In a paragraph from a case regarding negligence, the topic sentence is in another place. The case involves a gasoline drum that exploded and injured the driver of a tractor. The bung cap on the drum was badly worn from constant use and when the driver attempted to open it, a spark resulted and the gasoline drum exploded.

> The drum, or gasoline container, involved herein was of standard material, construction and manufacture, and of the kind in general use; and had it been in reasonably good repair there would, of course, be no liability. But the proof is that the drum had been in use nine years; that the threads in the bung plug or bung cap were broken, bent and jagged; that this condition had been brought about by

[1] *Flamm v. Van Nierop*, 56 Misc.2d 1059, 291 N.Y.S. 2d 189 (1968).

repeated hammering on the bung cap during the course of its use—a condition which had attracted the attention of one of appellants' employees before the container was sent out on this occasion. There is no adequate proof to show that appellee had equal knowledge or appreciation of the significance of this fact. . . . [Citation omitted]. *The proof is sufficient to show that a person of ordinary prudence, and mindful of the duty of cautious care with which appellants were charged, should have known of the condition aforesaid and should reasonably have anticipated as a likelihood of weight and moment, that a sudden fire or explosion would be caused by the stated condition of unrepair; and hence appellants are liable for the injury to appellee which resulted.*[2]

In this paragraph the topic sentence is last. It summarizes and concludes all that precedes it. The advantage of this placement is that it helps to reinforce the position established by the analysis. It serves not only as a signpost, but as a concluding signpost. It helps leave the impression that the conclusion is drawn from a definite, specific, and careful argument.

A third paragraph has still another place for the topic sentence. In this case a mentally deranged patient hit her nurse with a table leg. The nurse, who knew of the patient's mental illness and had gone in to calm her, sued for the injuries that she received.

On April 19, 1932, the defendant, while locked in her room, had a violent attack. The plaintiff heard a crashing of furniture and then knew that the defendant was ugly, violent, and dangerous. The defendant told the plaintiff and a Miss Maroney, "the maid," who was with the plaintiff in the adjoining room, that if they came into the defendant's room, she would kill them. The plaintiff and Miss Maroney looked into the defendant's room, "saw what the defendant had done," and "thought it best to take the broken stuff away before she did any harm to herself with it." They sent for a Mr. Emerton, the defendant's brother-in-law. When he arrived the defendant was in the middle of her room about ten feet from the door, holding upraised the leg of a low-boy as if she were going to strike. The plain-

---

[2] *Gulf Refining Co. v. Williams*, 183 Miss. 723, 185 So. 234 (1938).

tiff stepped into the room and walked toward the defendant, while Mr. Emerton and Miss Maroney remained in the doorway. As the plaintiff approached the defendant and tried to take hold of the defendant's hand which held the leg, the defendant struck the plaintiff's head with it, causing the injuries for which the action was brought.[3]

In this paragraph no single sentence summarizes all of the others. That doesn't mean there is no topic sentence; instead it means that the topic sentence is implied. A sentence can be written that will summarize the paragraph, but the writer might have decided not to include it to avoid repetition. In this paragraph a topic sentence could be: "The defendant, while having a violent attack, threatened and subsequently struck and injured the plaintiff." Including that sentence in the paragraph, however, would have only been awkward and repetitious.

There is also one other common place for a topic sentence. The following paragraph is from a case in which one man talked another into jumping into a ditch. Bigan, a coal mine operator, asked Yania, a competitor visiting Bigan's premises on business, to help start a pump. To help, Yania jumped into the trench full of water and was drowned.

Appellant initially contends that Yania's descent from the high embankment into the water and the resulting death were caused "entirely" by the spoken words and blandishments of Bigan delivered at a distance from Yania. The complaint does not allege that Yania slipped or that he was pushed or that Bigan made any physical impact upon Yania. On the contrary, the only inference deducible from the facts alleged in the complaint is that Bigan, by the employment of cajolery and inveiglement, caused such a mental impact on Yania that the latter was deprived of his volition and freedom of choice and placed under a compulsion to jump into the water. Had Yania been a child of tender years or mentally deficient then it is conceivable that taunting and enticement could constitute actionable negligence if it resulted in harm. However, to contend that such conduct directed to an adult in full possession of all his mental

---

[3] *McGuire v. Almy*, 297 Mass. 323, 8 N.E.2d 760 (1937).

faculties constitutes actionable negligence is not only without precedent but completely without merit. [Citation omitted].[4]

Here it may be convenient to think of the topic sentence as having two parts: the first sentence is a statement of the issue, and the last sentence is a conclusion or summary of the issue. This is often a good way to think of a topic sentence, especially in law examinations. Consider the following example, in which the first sentence of the paragraph states the issue, and the second part of the topic sentence, the last sentence in the paragraph, summarizes the argument.

> The first issue in this case of false imprisonment is whether the plaintiff was confined [body of paragraph omitted]. Therefore, since the plaintiff was not free to leave there was confinement.

Taken together, the two sentences summarize the whole paragraph and the whole issue.

The reason for breaking the topic sentence into two parts is that you have to identify the issue early in the paragraph, but you don't want to start with a conclusion. That is, you don't want to start by saying:

> X will collect from Y for X's injuries.

The reader wants to watch you come to that conclusion through your reasoning. To leave out the last sentence, however, would make the paragraph incomplete. And to add another sentence after your conclusion would be anticlimactic. Ordinarily, in a law exam, you should introduce the issue in the first sentence and summarize or conclude in the last sentence of each paragraph.

Paragraph Development

Now, what do those instructors mean who write "Needs development" in the margin of your paper beside your favorite para-

[4] *Yania v. Bigan*, 397 Pa. 316, 155 A.2d 343 (1959).

graph? They mean that you did not fulfill the promise of your topic sentence. You didn't prove your point. In both general persuasive and legal writing it usually means that you didn't support your conclusion. This is a very common problem in all writing, but it is especially grievous in legal writing. When you have worked on that hypothetical question long enough, you will have arrived at some conclusions well before you begin to write. But you still have to show the reader your reasoning process and justify your conclusion. Consider the following paragraph.

> The deceased, Homer, also had a relationship with Beatrice, who may claim a share of the estate. The rule states that only the living legal wife and legitimate children will inherit. Therefore, Beatrice will inherit part of Homer's estate.

In this paragraph the issue was stated, and the rule was given, but some facts and reasoning were missing. Whether Beatrice has yet been established as Homer's living legal wife has to be stated as the link leading to the conclusion that she may inherit. All the links must be there.

This same paragraph also might have been written with the fact included but the rule left out.

> The deceased, Homer, also had a relationship with Beatrice, who may claim a share of his estate. Since Beatrice married Homer in a civil ceremony, and since no other valid marriage was in existence, she is the legal wife. Therefore, Beatrice will inherit part of Homer's estate.

Sometimes, because the reasoning may seem apparent to you, you may state conclusions based on an unstated assumption. Instead, force yourself to include every step in the argument.

Paragraph Content

Your outline itself can help you make sure you have enough support in your paragraph, especially if you remember to use the proleptical method, that is, anticipate counterarguments. You can also ask yourself some helpful questions about the paragraph. Have counterarguments been considered and resolved? Have all the implications of your position been dealt with? Have you given specific reasons that show how you have arrived at that position? Finally, of course, the completeness of a paragraph in persuasive writing can only be measured by its effectiveness in supporting a single point or issue. Therefore, you should be very careful in establishing the topic of your paragraph so that it will be limited enough and specific enough to be handled in that small space.

Paragraph Organization

Some of the standard ways of organizing paragraphs are by example, description, chronology, definition, analogy, cause and effect, and inductive and deductive logic. Any of these methods of organizing paragraphs can be very effective in furthering an argument, but in legal analysis it is important to keep the focus on step-by-step progression through the issue. Readers generally prefer paragraphs that are fairly short, so it will be best to identify the point you are making, address the point, and move on.

Note that a discussion of any single issue may take several paragraphs, so don't try to compress all of your discussion of each issue into single paragraphs.

Transition within the Paragraph

In a way, a paragraph is automatically unified if all of the sentences deal with the same subject. But for it to sound unified, you must consciously think of making smooth transition from one sentence to the next.

Compare the following two paragraphs.

1. Jones may bring an action for battery against Smith to recover for his injuries. Jones was struck in the nose by Smith, and Jones's nose was injured. A battery is a harmful or offensive touching of another that is intentional, unprivileged, and unconsented. Smith thought Jones had said something insulting to him. Smith does not have justification for striking Jones. The touch was unprivileged, unconsented, and harmful. Jones will recover from Smith for his injuries.
2. Jones may bring an action for battery against Smith to recover for his injuries. *His injuries* were incurred when

Jones was struck in the nose by Smith. *The rule to be applied to this situation is that* a battery is the unconsented, unprivileged, harmful, or offensive touching of another. *Even though* Smith thought Jones had said something offensive to him, *that is* not enough justification for striking Jones. *Since* the striking was *therefore* unprivileged and unconsented, and *since* it was harmful, Jones will recover from Smith for his injuries.

What we have done in paragraph 2 is add transitions to show how the sentences relate to one another. When you do this, you reinforce the unity of your paragraph.

Of course there is another element to transition, and that is logic. The logic of your argument helps ensure flow and smooth shifts from one sentence to the next in your paragraph. Logic leads you from one premise to the next and finally to the conclusion.

SENTENCE STRUCTURE

As we suggested at the beginning of this chapter, the kinds of writing difficulties most law and prelaw students have are not strictly grammatical. In one sense, "grammatical" simply means "according to the system"—the system being that largely unconscious knowledge of language that is possessed by every native speaker of a language. It is what allows you to speak and understand sentences in your own language. In this sense of the word, almost any sentence that you might say or write will be perfectly grammatical because producing sentences is a part of the linguistic ability possessed by you and every other speaker of a language.

There is another, narrower sense of the word "grammatical" that most people have perhaps come to think of as its primary or even its *only* meaning. According to this sense of the word, "grammatical" means something like "in conformity with traditional rules of good usage." These "rules of good usage" are in some cases legitimate reflections of the actual system of English; in other cases they are completely arbitrary prescriptions often based on little more than the whim of some eighteenth-century schoolmaster.

As we see it, the problem is not so much one of using "good grammar" as it is one of employing language appropriate to the audience. Usage that would be appropriate in conversation might not be appropriate in some kinds of writing. And it is no secret that legal writing has a certain formality about it. We don't, however, wish to push this too far and insist on some rigid pattern of usage that resounds with overtones of decorum, formality, and perhaps even snobbishness or, at the other extreme, obsequiousness. Instead, we suggest that rather than worrying about the way you generate sentences from thought to paper, rather than being concerned with an analysis of verb placement or noun clusters, the more profitable way of improving your writing at the basic sentence level is to become aware of the faulty sentences you are most likely to write. If we can help you eliminate sentences that might be awkward or unclear and replace them with sentences that don't violate even the prescriptive grammars, your writing can be improved immediately.

Effective Sentences

We can identify two major elements in effective sentences. First, an effective sentence is one that conveys your thoughts clearly. Second, an effective sentence conveys to the reader a sense of confidence in you, the writer.

One test of an effective sentence is that it expresses your thoughts so that a reader can grasp them immediately. To help you ensure that your sentences meet this test, we are going to point out the most common problems that make sentences ineffective. This approach may sound negative at first. We might have been concerned in this chapter with a quest for the elusive "perfect sentence," and here we are just trying to help you avoid imperfect ones. But by eliminating these errors, you can improve your writing markedly.

A second test of an effective sentence is that it gives the reader a sense of confidence in the writer. Many readers, including law professors, senior partners in law firms, and judges, consciously or unconsciously make judgments about the writer based on language usage. In addition to a concern with logical argument and mental processes, judgments often are based on whether words are spelled correctly, commas are placed in the right position, and periods are put only at the end of true sentences. (Given these multiple criteria for judgment, your most immediate task probably is to learn to avoid those grammatical errors that lessen your credibility.

In this chapter, we will identify and discuss the most common problems at the sentence level. Also, we will again encourage you to spend a couple of minutes proofreading your papers or answers after you have written them to check for sentence problems.

Sentence Problems

Right now we just want to emphasize the glaring errors in sentence construction, the ones that make some instructors roll their eyes and look up from their papers in despair, the ones that label the writer "weak" or—well, you can supply your own pejoratives. We will treat seven major sentence level problems that we have found in more papers than we like to remember. And to help you avoid each problem, we will discuss the reasons they are committed.

Sentence Fragments.   Sometimes just writing a complete sentence is a problem. Because much of our conversation is made up of words and phrases that communicate perfectly well but that cannot be, or might not be, punctuated as complete sentences, we are all tempted to use the same language in writing.

> Italian food?
> Sounds great!
> Joe's?
> Sure.

In conversation or writing, this exchange would be perfectly clear. Unfortunately, some conversations would not be clear when written because writing consists only of words and punctuation. No gestures or variations in intonation, volume, or timing are available to reinforce or complete the meaning of the words. Therefore, the writer, to be clear, has to be as complete as possible.

There is also another concern. Many people have a strong prejudice against the sentence fragment. Whether they have sound linguistic reasons or whether they only had exceptionally effective early indoctrination, they abhor this particular linguistic phenomenon. Consequently, it would be just as well to avoid sentence fragments. And a good way to avoid them is to understand what causes them.

Appended Phrases and Clauses.   One major reason for occasionally ending up with a sentence fragment is that one subidea is added to a major idea by a dependent clause punctuated as a sentence.

> The plaintiff can bring suit for negligence against the city for the injuries he sustained in the accident. *Even though his contributory negligence may bar him from recovery.*

In this example the sentence itself, the major idea, was written first. Then the student decided to qualify his statement by adding the subidea that begins with "Even though. . . ." Together, the two thoughts read as a single sentence. Unfortunately, they have been punctuated as two.

A way to check for this common slip is, while proofreading, to be alert to sentences that begin with words like *since, because, if, whether or not, even though,* and *although.* Read through those sentences separately to make sure they aren't dependent clauses, that is, that they don't depend on a previous or subsequent independent clause to form a complete sentence.

Omission of Verb or Subject. Sometimes in long and involved sentences, the subject or the verb gets left out. This usually happens as a writer stops to think midway in the sentence and loses track of the structure he or she first had in mind.

> Under the impression that a crime was being committed, hearing the shots, struck the bystander over the head. [subject omitted]

One very good way to protect yourself from this problem is to keep your sentences fairly short and direct. This doesn't mean that you should write in classic third-grade style. It does mean that if you discover that you sometimes lose track of subject or verb, you should avoid those intricate, multiqualified sentences that are full of interdependent clauses. As a matter of fact, even if you don't lose track, you should avoid those kinds of sentences in legal writing. Instructors can get very impatient if every thought is overqualified and underclarified.

Run-on Sentences. As a former professor of ours used to say, you not only have to write complete sentences, you have to write them one at a time.

There are two major kinds of run-on sentences. First, there are those in which two potentially complete sentences are written as one with no punctuation. These are also known as (a.k.a.) fused sentences.

> He might not have run the stop light it might not have been working.

Second, there are those run-on sentences (a.k.a. comma splices) in which two potentially complete sentences are joined by a comma.

> The woman was frightened by the man she described as seedy, it was only after she struck him with a rock that she discovered he was an undercover policeman.

The major problem with both fused sentences and comma splices is lack of clarity. Inappropriate punctuation can often be misleading or confusing.

> The robber fled on foot leaving his loot as he turned the corner the victim took up the chase.

Here it is impossible to tell if the loot was left on the corner, or if the victim just took up the chase then. The insertion of a period or semicolon would clarify the writer's intention.

Even when the writer separates potentially complete sentences with commas, there is a chance for misreading the sentence.

> The officer fell off the bridge while directing traffic, according to the official report, he may have been on his way home from the Policeman's Ball.

In this example it isn't clear if the official report indicated that the policeman was directing traffic or that he had just come from the ball.

To help avoid these problems, be as clear as possible by separating complete thoughts (independent clauses). Make them separate sentences, or use a semicolon or a connective word or phrase.

Subject/Verb Agreement.   Another sentence problem that smacks of traditional grammar rules but has very current and practical application is lack of agreement between subject and verb. The most common violation of this principle is with agreement in number. Subject and verb should agree in form—that is, if the subject is singular, the verb should be singular; if the subject is plural, the verb should be plural.

> He *files* an action.
> They *file* an action.

That seems easy enough because the alternatives ("he file" and "they files") don't sound right. But in longer sentences where there are words and clauses that separate the subject from the verb, confusion is easy. This is another good reason for keeping your sentences short. Some types of sentences, because of their structure, make it less easy to assure subject/verb agreement.

Intervening Nouns. When another noun of a different number comes between the subject and verb, it is sometimes tempting to use the wrong verb form.

This manufacturer, like most firms, (provide/*provides*) only partial warranty.

The subject of the sentence is "manufacturer," not "firms," so the verb should be "provides," and not "provide." But the intervening noun may be confusing. If you are in doubt, try to simplify the sentence in your mind by isolating the subject and verb. Eliminate the phrase ("like most firms") until you get to the core of the sentence: "This manufacturer provides only a partial warranty."

Sometimes, though, it isn't easy to identify the subject.

One of the corporate lawyers (*is*/are) best qualified to answer that question.

If "one" is the subject, the verb should be "is." If "lawyers" is the subject, the verb should be "are." In the construction "One of the corporate lawyers," the prepositional phrase ("of the corporate lawyers") plays no part in determining the form of the verb. "One" is the subject, so "is" is the verb.

Indefinite Pronouns. A similar problem occurs when the subject of a sentence is an indefinite pronoun such as *either, neither, each, every,* or *everyone.*

Neither of the parties to the action (*was*/were) in favor of settling out of court.
Each of the purchasers (*was*/were) *aware* of the defect.

All you have to remember, though, is that *each* of these words *is* singular in form. (Think of them as "each one," or "neither one.") Then just use the singular form of the verb.

Compound Subjects.   Subjects that are joined by "and" become compound subjects and require a plural verb.

The plaintiff and the defendant (*agree*/agrees) in principle.
Drinking homemade liquor and fighting in pool halls (*bring*/brings) both civil and criminal liabilities.

Correlative Subjects.   The problem becomes a little more difficult when the subjects are not joined by "and" but by "either . . . or," "neither . . . nor," "not only . . . but," and like constructions.

Neither the prosecution nor the defendants (is/*are*) happy with the jury selected.
Not only the bystanders but the policeman (*was*/were) convinced a crime was in progress.

The general rule is that the verb should agree with the part of the subject closest to it. The sentence seems to sound better that way, and in any case, if you use the italicized word it won't be incorrect.

Ambiguous Modifiers.   A sentence as a whole may contain a great deal of information that it conveys to the reader. The information can be muddled, though, because of some ambiguity in a misplaced modifier—a word or phrase that describes or gives additional information. The rule is simple: keep the modifier by that which it modifies. Unfortunately, there are many times when the modifier gets added to the sentence as an afterthought. Instead of adding information then, it only obscures the reference.

Some states hold that one is not responsible for his acts in certain situations, such as Alabama.

You can see that the modifying phrase "such as Alabama" should be inserted between "Some states" and "hold." This modifier has just been placed next to the wrong word.
In other sentences, modifiers may not be placed by the wrong word but may be interpreted as modifying the wrong part of the sentence.

Due to a sudden negligent stop, under a New York statute, the railroad company has strict liability.

The image of a train stopped under a New York statute is intriguing, but writers have to be sensitive to any possible misreading of their sentences. Modifiers have to be placed not only so that they modify the appropriate word or phrase, but so that they modify *only* that word or phrase.

Often the result of a misplaced modifier is humorous, but it can be serious. Legal writing has to be precise, and if a sentence can be interpreted in any way other than the way you intended it, you can be sure someone will read it that way.

Ambiguous Pronouns. Pronouns can be ambiguous to the reader in two ways. First, with personal pronouns the reader may not be able to understand who is being referred to by the pronoun. Although it is very convenient to use pronouns to avoid repeating names, writers have to repeat them enough times so that the reader can keep straight the pronoun reference.

Crummy told Nasty that he should not have taken the leash.

The store detective questioned John as he was waiting for the elevator.

Here, we don't know who took the leash or who was waiting for the elevator. It is better to be a little repetitious than to be ambiguous. Go ahead and repeat the name if there is any chance that the pronoun can be taken to refer to the wrong person.

Crummy told Nasty that Nasty should not have taken the leash.

The store detective questioned John as John was waiting for the elevator.

Second, with pronouns like *this, that, which,* and *it,* a different kind of ambiguity can occur. When they are used to refer to some large or vague concept and not to a specific term, the reference may be unclear.

The man who took the leash from Mr. Kent did so in an offensive manner, *which* was clearly a battery.

Although the witness claimed that he called the police immediately after seeing the defendant assault the plaintiff, the defendant claims that *it* isn't true.

In the first example, "which" has no particular referent in the first part of the sentence. In the second example, "it" could refer to the immediacy of the call or to the assault. As a rule, use pronouns only to refer clearly to specific nouns.

Parallel Structure.   One other common writing problem at the sentence level occurs when there is a lack of parallel structure. Sentences lacking parallel structure are subject to two problems. First, the sentences may just sound awkward.

    a. The First Amendment protects freedom of speech, freedom of assembly, and the press is required to be unfettered.
    b. The plaintiff claimed that the defendant was striking him, kicked him, and ran away.

To make your sentence structure parallel, you have to make sure that all of the elements in your sentence have the same form. When you have items in a series, any discrepancy is especially obvious. But you don't need a set of rules regarding parallel infinitives, participial phrases, and so on, to maintain parallel structure. You can probably just listen to the sentences and tell that it sounds better to write the following.

    a. The First Amendment protects freedom of speech, freedom of assembly, and freedom of the press.
    b. The plaintiff claimed that the defendant struck him, kicked him, and ran away.

The second problem is that without parallel structure, your writing could be repetitious. Using parallelism keeps you from having to repeat similar sentence elements.

The waiter yelled at Mrs. Trueblue. He also insulted her. Furthermore, the waiter abused Mrs. Trueblue.

The problem is a little obvious in this example, but even obvious problems occur with surprising frequency. Using parallel structure, the three sentences can be written as follows.

The waiter insulted, abused, and yelled at Mrs. Trueblue.

Your sentences may not be any more profound, but parallel structure can help you avoid repetition and awkwardness.

Shifted Constructions. The same reason we all sometimes end up with nonparallel constructions, verbs and subjects that don't agree, sentence fragments, and a humbling number of sentences that are awkward or mystifying is that we "shift" somewhere in the sentence. We may start with one construction in mind, but when inspiration strikes, we take off in that new direction, enlightened and optimistic, heedless of where we are or where we were going.

a. Even though speeding is held to be negligent in New York the fact that Adams was speeding and committed a negligent act, he is not liable because the statute exempts him from liability to guests.

b. Depriving a person of something closely associated with his person constitutes a harmful act by intentionally depriving Kent of his Seeing Eye dog by grabbing the leash out of Kent's hands.

In these two examples, the writers had a thought in mind when they began to write, but by the middle of both sentences they had become confused and just tried to write their way out of the sentence. If you get confused, don't try to write your way out of the sentence; you'll just get into more trouble. Start over. Separate your thoughts and state them separately.

CONCLUSION

If you can prevent these potential paragraph and sentence level problems in your own papers, you can at least make sure that your writing isn't diminished by any cosmetic errors. In addition, you will probably improve the substance of your writing. That is, often these sentence errors are the product of confused thinking on your part. In attempting to straighten out the ambiguities in your sentences, you may well eliminate the ambiguities in your thinking.

EXERCISE IN THE MECHANICS OF LEGAL WRITING

Identify the errors in the sentences below: (F) fragment, (RO) run-on, (SV) incorrect subject/verb agreement, (AM) ambiguous modifier, (AP) ambiguous pronoun, (P) lack of parallel structure, (SC) shifted construction. Correct the errors. See the Appendix for answers.

1. Alvin was falsely imprisoned in the moving van although he was not aware of his confinement, he was harmed by it.
2. Under California law drivers are liable to their guests when they have been negligent.
3. With his insulting words and when he abused her, he exceeded all bounds that decent society would tolerate.
4. Mrs. Gordon's car was parked on the railroad tracks and would therefore be liable to Mr. Smith.
5. The outcome of these suits depend heavily on the state the action is filed in.
6. Because, the plaintiff did not see the blow coming.
7. Fighting in the street, the police were forced to arrest the men.
8. The contract, only verbal, without even any witnesses.
9. Neither of the victims were injured.
10. Where the conduct is outrageous or in similar situations of intentional infliction of emotional distress.
11. After the suspect was stopped for speeding, the police searched the car and then they let him go. This was obviously unfair.
12. While the plaintiff can only bring an action in the state of California.
13. The lawyer and his clients disagrees.
14. Defendant accosted Mrs. Bates while she was walking in the park in a most offensive manner.
15. There was a fence around the pool. Whether or not there was a lock on the gate.
16. Lastly, the claim that the defendant was speeding.
17. Driving at a high rate of speed, the statute makes the defendant liable.
18. The reason being that she caused the car to swerve.

19. Notwithstanding its many shortcomings, this court has adopted the Missouri rule.
20. Congress should have the power to enforce the provisions of this article, which is another issue.
21. The question is whether the bank will be able to recover from Harry for a loan made by Wanda, his wife, under false pretenses.
22. They stopped the assault when the dog attacked, which relieved the victim.
23. Although it did not happen in that particular state.
24. The federal officers arrived at the conclusion that a felony was being committed by the odor of moonshine whiskey.
25. I'm unsure of all the elements in false imprisonment, but this is not really an issue.
26. If it can be proven that the automobile was defective and it was the manufacturer's fault.

CHAPTER EIGHT
Legal Writing Style

INTRODUCTION

Over the last few years, we have seen a major movement emphasizing "plain English" in legal writing. And it has not just been the popular press or the confused layman calling for change. Lawyers, judges, and law professors are equally concerned over the style of obfuscation and muddy prose that has too often been associated with legal writing. The style even has a name: legalese.

In the first chapter of *Plain English for Lawyers,* Richard Wydick writes

> We lawyers cannot write plain English. We use eight words to say what could be said in two. We use arcane phrases to express commonplace ideas. Seeking to be cautious, we become verbose. Our sentences twist on, phrase within clause within clause glazing the eyes and numbing the minds of our readers.[1]

---

[1] Richard Wydick, *Plain English for Lawyers,* 2nd ed. (Carolina Academic Press, Durham, North Carolina, 1985), p. 3.

Plain English laws have been established in some states. Books and articles advise on ways of writing contracts, pleadings, and other kinds of legal documents in plain English. In the first two editions of this text we have argued for clear, direct, uninflated writing for lawyers and law students. Maybe we just have to emphasize the point even more in law schools.

Too many law students are tempted to imitate what they think is legal language. For too many, there seems to be an almost irresistible urge to clothe everything in the diction and style of the most incomprehensible insurance policy. The truth is that most legal writing isn't that formulistic and stylized at all. And certainly most writing assignments in law school don't call for rigid formality. The language that students are asked to use in analyzing fact situations is not the language of stereotypical contracts or insurance policies, yet many students seem unable to resist trying to make their exam answers read that way.

There probably is such a thing as legal style, though it is not as stiff as the beginning student might imagine. Much legal writing is impersonal and somewhat formal, but when it is done well, it is not stilted. Above all, it is a style that should be acquired naturally by reading enormous amounts of good legal prose, and not by conscious, forced imitation. Students must also be critical readers. It may sound like heresy, but not all judicial opinions are well written. Our goal in this chapter is to help you achieve the very best legal writing style, and that is a clear, precise expression of ideas written in plain English.

THE NATURE OF STYLE

Some think of style as the kind of flair a writer has. Others take it to mean some dramatic rhetorical tricks one can play with. Still others, extrapolating from what is found in "style sheets," think it is putting commas in the correct places. Some see style as something everyone has, and others see it as something to be attained. We think of it as a term to describe the writer's stance and voice—a manner of address. Style has to do with choice of words, with choice of sentence length and structure, and with the pattern of ideas in writing. We also recognize that each of us has an individual writing style that is an expression of our attitudes and personalities.

Not all styles are equally pleasing or useful. Some are too breezy, some too heavy, some dull, some just annoying. In this chapter, we are going to emphasize a style that is clear, direct, and straightforward.

A Good Style

A good style is characterized by diction that is appropriate to the audience and occasion and that is lively and direct. Sentences are balanced and varied in structure. Ideas are related to each other, and transition from one to the next is smooth. Altogether, the writing is pleasing in itself as it expresses the writer's ideas.

While we think this is a fair description, just try to develop a good style by reference to that paragraph. It would be pretty futile. However, we aren't primarily interested in helping you develop an abstractly correct prose style. Nor do we offer an elaborate apparatus to distinguish style. You may have seen one of the complex statistical methods of stylistic analysis. Though they might be useful for some language studies, we don't find them helpful for our purposes.

Our goal is to help you refine your own style so that you can assert yourself clearly and compellingly. You will have to avoid stylistic flaws, those problems that clog sentence flow and detract from the substance of your ideas. Also, as you progress through this chapter and through your own papers, you will have to be conscious of sentence structure and your choice of words. Finally, you will have to be ruthless in editing your work if you find that you indulge in one of the bad habits we identify as detracting from good style.

Varieties of Style

You probably already have different writing styles, depending on your audience or purpose. You may be casual and free in a personal letter, but formal and controlled in a school assignment. Style is more than level of usage, although that aspect is important. You do have to consider your audience. The trouble with thinking too much about levels of usage is that you might become so conscious of the formality of an occasion, such as a law school assignment, that you write in an unnatural, forced way and end up with contorted prose. You will find some examples of overly elevated writing later in this chapter.

But even in the best legal writing there are various kinds of styles. Judges write their decisions in styles ranging from *severely formal* to *direct and plain.*

In the following paragraph from an appellate decision, the style is quite formal, and, in fact, the same allegations might have been stated much more simply by other judges.

> In this case the parents of an injured child sue the parents of a boy who had beaten their son. They claimed that the parents should have exercised more control over their son since they knew he sometimes harmed smaller children.
>
> The allegations in the complaint, taken at their face value, show notice to the parents of the dangerous propensities of their minor son, an ability to control him in that regard and a complete default in restraining him from conduct calculated to harm others which by reason of his prior antics could reasonably have been anticipated. The parents therefore owed a duty to society to guard their son closely to see to it that he did not indulge in his vicious propensities.[2]
>
> [The court found for the parents of the injured child.]

The next paragraph is written in a plain and direct style by Justice Cardozo. The facts of the case are described by the Justice.

> Plaintiff and his cousin Herbert boarded a car at a station near the bottom of one of the trestles. Other passengers, entering at the same time, filled the platform, and blocked admission to the aisle. The platform was provided with doors but the conductor did not close them. Moving at from 6 to 8 miles an hour, the car, without slackening, turned the curve. There was a violent lurch, and Herbert Wagner was thrown out, near the point where the trestle changes to a bridge. The cry was raised, "man overboard." The car went across the bridge and stopped near the foot of the incline. Night and darkness had come on. Plaintiff

---

[2] *Linder v. Binder,* 50 Misc.2d 320, 270 N.Y.S. 2d 427 (1966).

walked along the trestle, a distance of 445 feet, until he arrived at the bridge where he thought to find his cousin's body. He says that he was asked to go there by the conductor. He says, too, that the conductor followed with a lantern. Both these statements the conductor denies. Several other persons, instead of ascending the trestle, went beneath it, and discovered under the bridge the body they were seeking. As they stood there, the plaintiff's body struck the ground beside them. Reaching the bridge, he had found upon a beam his cousin's hat, but nothing else. About him there was darkness. He missed his footing, and fell.[3] [A new trial was granted and plaintiff was allowed to sue for negligence.]

One other example of style is from a delightful decision written by Justice Carlin of New York. This decision is not meant as an example of the clear, direct style we advocate for law students, but only as an illustration of the range of writing styles to be found in the law. In his decision, Justice Carlin employed a mock-heroic style as he narrated the adventures of a cab driver whose taxi was commandeered by a robber. The cab driver bailed out, and the taxi struck three pedestrians. The issue is whether the cab driver should have stayed with his cab despite the danger.

This case presents the ordinary man—that problem child of the law—in a most bizarre setting. As a lonely chauffeur in defendant's employ he became in a trice the protagonist in a breath-bating drama with a denouement almost tragic. It appears that a man, whose identity it would be indelicate to divulge, was feloniously relieved of his portable goods by two nondescript highwaymen in an alley near 26th Street and Third Avenue, Manhattan; they induced him to relinquish his possessions by a strong argument *ad hominem* couched in the convincing cant of the criminal and pressed at the point of a most persuasive pistol. Laden with their loot, but not thereby impeded, they took an abrupt departure and he, shuffling off the coil of that discretion which enmeshed him in the alley, quickly gave chase through 26th Street toward 2nd Avenue, whither they were resorting

---

[3] *Wagner v. International Railway Co.*, 232 N.Y. 176, 133 N.E. 437 (1921).

"with expedition swift as thought" for most obvious reasons. Somewhere on that thoroughfare of escape they indulged the stratagem of separation ostensibly to disconcert their pursuer and allay the ardor of his pursuit. He then centered on for capture the man with the pistol, whom he saw board the defendant's taxicab, which quickly veered south toward 25th Street on 2nd Avenue, where he saw the chauffeur jump out while the cab, still in motion, continued toward 24th Street; after the chauffeur relieved himself of the cumbersome burden of his fare the latter also is said to have similarly departed from the cab before it reached 24th Street. . . .

The chauffeur—the ordinary man in this case—acted in a split second in a most harrowing experience. To call him negligent would be to brand him a coward; the court does not do so in spite of what those swaggering heroes, "whose valor plucks dead lions by the beard," may bluster to the contrary. The court is loathe to see the plaintiffs go without recovery even though their damages were slight, but cannot hold the defendant liable upon the facts adduced at the trial. Motions, upon which decision was reserved, to dismiss the complaint are granted, with exceptions to plaintiffs. Judgment for defendant against plaintiffs dismissing their complaint upon the merits.[4]

We use these examples from well-written decisions to show that there is a whole spectrum of styles acceptable in legal writing. There is an almost equally broad spectrum in law schools. Students have been successful using any number of prose styles—familiar and formal, loose and balanced—all flavored with idiosyncrasy. We are not going to try to lead you into a particular prose style, but instead we will try to help you improve your own, using the same procedures as in the chapter on mechanics. Instead of hunting that elusive "good sentence" or "good style," we will identify stylistic flaws that could mar your writing. We proceed on the assumption that if you can just clean up your own style, the clarity of your expression will then depend on the clarity of your thinking. It will not be garbled in the translation from thought to written language.

[4] *Cordas v. Peerless Transportation Co.*, 27 N.Y.S.2d 198 (1941).

STYLISTIC FLAWS

Naturally, as a law student you will want to write something that sounds important, maybe even profound. But in trying to create that memorable answer that allows you to feel as though you are walking hand in hand with Justice Cardozo, you might end up with only a curiously distorted and obscure paper.

Inflated Diction

One reason for a possible failure is the use of inflated diction. A major element of style is diction—choice of words—and some misguided law students sometimes try to choose not the most natural word, or even the most exact, but the *longest.* These students stretch their vocabularies beyond the limit of elasticity to try to make their statements sound important. Remarkable sentences result.

In an answer to a family law question, a student wrote

> Due to the deceased's many elongated affairs, the problems of heredity become complex.

The student meant "prolonged" instead of "elongated," and "inheritance" rather than "heredity."

The problem in the example is especially clear because some words were misused. But even when vocabulary is used more accurately, elevated language doesn't always make the writing sound better; it is much more likely to make the writer sound pompous and slightly ridiculous.

> Owing to the impecunious state of the defendant, he, with onerous force, assailed the plaintiff.

That same sentence, stated in more colloquial terms, might read

> Because the defendant was flat broke, he beat the living daylights out of the plaintiff.

Of course, neither version is appropriate for legal writing; the first is too stilted, the second too colloquial.

You may ask, "Well, what's wrong with using a bigger word as long as it's used correctly?" One problem is clarity. Strictly speaking, no two words have the same meaning. There are connotations that attach to language, and even two synonyms will suggest slightly different meanings to a reader. So, unless a student uses a particular term often and easily, he or she might be mistaken as to its precise usage.

For example, many students who have learned the term *res ipsa loquitur* ("the thing speaks for itself") misuse it immediately. While the term refers to a specific legal doctrine, students are tempted to use it in place of saying "It is obvious." To a lawyer or a law professor, this doesn't show eloquence but rather an inability to use legal language.

A second problem is simply stylistic. If your language sounds at all forced or awkward, instead of seeming more important, the writing will seem incompetent and inappropriate. Even though you may not have an elegant style, there is a certain grace in writing naturally that makes the material believable and adds force to the answer.

Inflated diction, then, leads to two possibilities: misuse of terms or correct use at an inappropriate time. Resist the temptation to elevate your language for the law; write in plain English.

Wordiness

A second kind of inflation relates not so much to the level of language but to its sheer bulk. The same impulse might be behind both kinds of inflation, though: a fear of sounding too simple.

> The issues which this tort case pose can result in significant differences regarding the legal distribution of liability among all involved parties depending upon the state in which legal action is brought and, accordingly, the law which is applied, ultimately.

You can imagine the writer of this sentence sitting back, heart filled with joy from having created half a paragraph from almost nothing. But, as King Lear says, "Nothing will come of nothing."

Two problems result from wordiness. First, you don't have the time to indulge in either an inflated or rambling approach to an analysis of issues. Because law school exams are both timed and complex, any misuse of those few minutes leaves even fewer to discuss too many issues.

Second, when there is too much verbiage in an answer, the reader tends to start skimming and skipping in search of the meat. If your crucial statement is nestled in the middle of a long, rambling paragraph, the reader may overlook it. Or if it is only implied by that long paragraph, you have to depend on the reader to do too much of the work in your answer.

Be economical. Short paragraphs and direct sentences will help you make the many points you have to make in law exams. This doesn't mean that you should just have a series of simple sentences. Obviously that would make you sound slightly simple yourself, and the reader would be a little worried about you. But you can learn to recognize wordiness by being sensitive to it.

First, decide if you're saying something in a roundabout way. Have you used abstract words when you should have been specific? Are you taking too many words to make your point, as in the example that began this section?

Second, notice if you have any "deadwood" in your sentences, words, or phrases that are redundant or useless.

It was the consensus *of opinion* that a reasonable man would not have acted in such a manner, *so to speak.*

Because "consensus" means "a collective opinion," the words "of opinion" are redundant. "So to speak" is just filler. Don't worry. By eliminating wordiness you won't regress to third-grade style.

Jargon

Jargon is specialized or technical language related to a particular activity or group of people. Doctors use terms among themselves that are foreign to the layperson, like "stat" ("right now") and "PRN" ("as needed"). Lawyers speak of "writs of mandamus" and "judgments n.o.v." Poker players have their own jargon ("jacksback") as do short-order cooks ("burn one" for a well-done hamburger). They all understand each other. Whenever a group of people have a particular profession or interest in common, jargon develops.

There is nothing wrong with jargon in that sense. The specialized language of any group is effective and clear within the group. However, there is not much justification for using it when the audience is not familiar with the terms. In legal writing, certain legal terms are not only acceptable but essential, and of course the reader will be familiar with the jargon. Principles of law (e.g., *res ipsa loquitur*), procedural matters (e.g., judgment notwithstanding the verdict), documents (e.g., summons), all have to be referred to by the proper terms.

But there are other aspects of jargon that are stylistically objectionable. Most of us have read documents written in government jargon or educational jargon that are totally incomprehensible. In those cases, proliferation of jargon concealed rather than revealed meaning. Sometimes jargon is even used to substitute for meaning. Try to keep these dangers in mind and use only that specialized language of the law that is necessary for accuracy in your writing. In other words, don't just plug in jargon to make your sentence sound "legal."

There is also jargon associated with legal writing that relates more to style than substance. Consider the following sentence.

> The above-named manufacturer is liable for all damages related to the crash and injuries sustained therein by the aforementioned parties.

Here the student who wrote the sentence seems less concerned with the substance of the statement than with the level of language. It has to sound "legal." This sentence may have sounded "legal" to that student, but instead it was just awkward. Take away the "aforementioneds" and "thereins" and some students are afraid they're back to "How I Spent My Summer Vacation."

Another bit of jargon we often see is the use of the word "said," as in "said incident" and "said judgment." It is this kind of jargon, superfluous and imposed on the sentence, that detracts from writing style and leads to the worst kind of legalese.

As implied earlier, another problem caused by jargon appears as soon as law students start learning some Latin terms. The temptation to use them to spice up their writing is almost irresistible. As soon as one student learned that *supra* means "above" and *infra* means "below," he wrote this sentence on his next exam.

> The defendant, as named *supra*, will be shown *infra* to be, as the facts indicate, liable for all damages.

If you are going to use any bit of legal jargon, make sure you use it accurately. Don't just come close.

Right: Smith has a *cause of action* in battery against Jones.
Wrong: Smith has a *course of action* in battery against Jones.
Wrong: Smith has a *causative action* in battery against Jones.

All of the faults listed *supra*—inflated diction, wordiness, and jargon—result from trying to sound important. However, there are a number of other stylistic flaws that are the result of habit rather than intention. Some examples follow.

Passives

The passive voice is a construction in which the subject is the receiver of the action. You have probably been told that the active voice, in which the subject performs the action of the sentence, is preferable.

Passive: The automobile *was damaged* by the driver.
Active: The driver *damaged* the automobile.
Passive: The plaintiff *was struck* by the defendant.
Active: The defendant *struck* the plaintiff.

Which construction you choose depends on whether you are more interested in the automobile or the driver, the plaintiff or defendant. If you are attorney for the plaintiff and want to call attention to him, you might very well refer to him first and end up with a passive construction.

The defendant, in turn, asks to recover for the extensive damage to his hand that resulted when the free movement of the defendant's right hand was impeded by plaintiff's nose.

However, we doubt that you'll be very successful even with that construction.
On the other hand there are times when the passive construction does work—for instance, when the actor is unknown.

The liquor store *was robbed* last night.
The shots *were fired* from a hill overlooking the freeway.

Thus, in some instances the passive construction works perfectly well. However, it is still true that generally the active voice is preferable because it is shorter, more direct, and usually more lively.

In legal writing, too many students overuse the passive construction, apparently because it seems impersonal and safe, and makes them feel more removed from the action.

In the situation where Jones is *tripped* by Smith, battery is *suggested* by the facts.

Perhaps students feel that with a passive construction, all of the facts and issues just appear and that the writers don't have to take personal responsibility for creating or discovering any issues. Or, perhaps they feel that by avoiding a direct statement they cannot be wrong. Unfortunately for them, the passive voice does not work that way.

The Passive Sense

But it is not just the true passive voice that weakens writing style. A similar construction has a passive effect, although, technically, it is not the passive voice.

When the striking of the plaintiff by the defendant *occurred,* the possibility of assault and battery *arose.*

With "occurred" and "arose," there is no action happening to the subjects of the verbs, and therefore it is not the passive voice; but there is a passive sense in the sentence that makes it unnecessarily weak.

Better: When the defendant struck the plaintiff, assault and battery became possible issues.

Issues and questions, like sea monsters, always just mysteriously arise. No one ever seems to do anything in these passive sentences. For each time there is a need for a passive construction, there are many more times when the reader would welcome a more straightforward statement. Use active verbs to enliven your sentences.

Abstractions

Just as the passive voice seems safer to some students, so too does abstraction. Abstractions result from being too vague and general in your writing. One kind of abstraction is evident when you use a general term when you really mean a specific one.

> General: If the *property* purchased by the decedent were to increase in value . . .
>
> Concrete: If the *stocks* purchased by the decedent were to increase in value . . .

Be specific. If you mean "knife," don't say "instrument." Otherwise you might be unintentionally ambiguous.

Another kind of abstraction results from generalizations. Some students may feel that if they make very general statements, they won't be challenged. Unfortunately, if that is true, it is true because they simply haven't said anything substantial enough for which to be challenged or rewarded. Generalizations are dangerous enough anyway, but in legal writing they can lead to disaster.

> Insulting another person in writing is cause for action in libel.

Whether this is just a misstatement of law or a careless generalization, the result is the same. Any conclusion based on that premise will be incorrect. The specific elements of libel must be identified and applied to the particular facts in question.

A similar kind of abstraction involves generalizations that are moral or ethical rather than strictly legal.

> To preserve those principles of justice and equality that have allowed our nation to remain free and strong, proper procedures of criminal investigation must be adhered to.

In classes on legal ethics and in some policy questions it is very important to explore moral implications of the law, but relying on philosophical abstractions to replace logical arguments will not work. Refer to the particular facts and rules by specific, concrete language.

The Interrogative Trap

A surprisingly large number of students have the habit of posing too many rhetorical questions in their writing. It may be a carryover from debate, where it is more useful, but it can be a problem in legal writing. When a question is rhetorical—a statement in interrogative form—it can become dangerous. We call the rhetorical question an interrogative trap because the writer just invites trouble by asking the reader anything. Most readers, and we are certainly among them, feel invited, maybe even compelled, to answer rhetorical questions in an essay. If you say "Why shouldn't the company be held responsible?" we immediately try to think of ten good reasons. And in doing so we may come upon an issue we think you should have discussed.

Rhetorical questions seem to invite negative responses. We hope it is not because we and our colleagues are naturally contrary, but rather because an assumption stated in such a smug way is not persuasive in a legal context.

Rhetorical question: Can there be any doubt that the act was intentional?

To that question we might instantly say, "Sure there can be, because . . ." In that case the writer had better be able to deal with any doubts he or she helped emphasize. But even if we were to agree with the conclusion, because a rhetorical question is a conclusion, the student is still obligated to support it. And too often rhetorical questions are used to suggest that there is no need for that support.

Although rhetorical questions are dangerous, the use of questions themselves in some contexts is fine. Many students start paragraphs with a question as the statement of the issue.

Is there a battery in this case?
Is the manufacturer liable for the injuries to A and B?

This usage is not a fault at all. It is not a trap because the question doesn't suggest extra issues. It is no better or worse than using a statement for identifying the issue.

> The issue is whether there is a battery in this case. A and B may bring an action against the manufacturer for their injuries.

Stating the issue as a question does specify the issue that is to be discussed in the paragraph. Posing a rhetorical question, however, may only raise other issues and invite unwanted response.

Clichés

A cliché is an overused expression that is consequently trite and ineffective. You probably already avoid many clichés, especially the automatic similes and metaphors.

> Happy as a lark.
> Slow as molasses.
> Colder than . . . (whatever is current)

An *effective* simile suggests a novel comparison between two things that reveals some unnoticed aspect of the subject. Clichés fail because they are no longer novel or fresh. Such similes and metaphors are easily avoided.

There are other clichés, though, that are harder to avoid because they are less forced. Some automatic phrases come too easily to mind, especially in highly structured, formal writing.

In a business letter many writers mechanically begin with "In re yours of the 21st . . . " because as the writer begins to write or dictate, that phrase is on the *tip of the tongue, so to speak.* In legal writing there are similar terms and phrases that *spring to mind* readily. And it is the automatic nature of these phrases that is objectionable, not the terms themselves.

Too often the phrase "cruel and unusual punishment" finds its way into an answer as a characterization of some calamitous event rather than in the appropriate constitutional context. And there are numerous similar terms you will use over and over in appropriate places. They become clichés, however, when they are used automatically without thought about their precise meanings.

A similar example occurs in discussions of battery. A battery is, in part, a "harmful or offensive touching." It is too apparent that many students just describe a touching in a fact situation as "harmful or offensive" without bothering to distinguish which term should apply, or whether both should apply. Clichés, then, can be substantively as well as stylistically harmful if they keep you from precise analysis and usage.

Try to express yourself without relying on clichés, legal or general. You don't have to propose brilliant similes and astonishingly apt metaphors; just use your own words.

Excessive Abbreviation

Many stylistic flaws occur more from carelessness than intention or habit. For some reason, maybe having to do with taking too many notes or briefing too many cases, law students rely heavily on abbreviation. K stands for Contract, π for Plaintiff, Δ for Defendant, and so forth. These and other symbols are sometimes acceptable even on exams (check with your instructors), but some students carry the practice to extremes. This sentence is taken from an examination on family law.

Big. makes mar. inv. Prior to Ten. recog. this mar., R m A in Ky. No valid mar. to M. Therefore M. no claim.

Perhaps the writer felt privy to some legal shorthand and wanted to show skill with it. But the resulting sentence is totally obscure. It looks like a fine word game, but since so many readers are poor sports, avoid excessive abbreviation.

If you have names in the fact situation that are just too long to repeat at each mention, at least write them out the first time you use them, and then write in parentheses the abbreviation you will use.

When Trebishovskolnin (T) entered the store . . .

On the other hand, if the names are short, don't abbreviate them. It will only get you into trouble. You and your reader have a much better chance of keeping "Robert" and "Kenneth" straight than you do of keeping (R) and (K) straight in your discussion.

Because a measure of good writing is effectiveness, write so that your reader will understand your references. Don't make the reader guess at your meaning because of excessive abbreviation.

Errors of Person

Grammatically, "person" refers to whoever is speaking, spoken to, or spoken about. The first person (I, we, us) is not usually used in legal writing because in an analysis of fact and law, it seems best to have the emphasis on the facts and the law, and not on the analyzer. It is a convention that makes legal writing a little more formal in style than other kinds of exposition, but law students should practice keeping themselves out of their answers.

> Weak: I think the question of sanity is important as we consider the defendant's intent.
>
> Better: The question of sanity is important in considering the defendant's intent.

Second person (you) is easily avoided because there is no specified person you will be writing to in an answer. Second person indefinite (a.k.a. the indefinite you) should also be avoided. This can be done simply by referring instead to the third person by name or pronoun.

> Weak: *You* can't run a stop sign without expecting to assume the risk.
>
> Better: *The defendant* could not have run the stop sign without expecting to assume the risk.

Avoiding the second person indefinite will also prevent the awkward shifts in person that are so common.

> Weak: This device prevents *drivers* who are intoxicated from starting their cars, because you can't remember the numbers when you're drunk.
>
> Better: This device prevents *drivers* who are intoxicated from starting their cars, because *they* can't remember the numbers when they're drunk.

Perhaps the most common shift in person in legal writing is one that occurs when students begin their answer in their own voice, develop it in the voice of their law professor, and conclude in the voice of Justice Cardozo. The writer goes from the first paragraph where he uses "I feel this is such and such," to a second paragraph that begins, "a court does such and such," and on to "this court therefore decrees. . . . " This maddening shift in persons leads the reader to believe that the writer has a minimum of six or eight personalities.

CONCLUSION

In working on your own prose style, be sensitive to any of the stylistic flaws that you may discover in your writing. Also, follow the few stylistic conventions of legal writing, such as using only third person. Finally, try to write naturally; that is, don't consciously try to affect a "legal style." Just smooth out your own. And, above all, avoid the awkwardness and artificiality of legalese.

EXERCISE IN LEGAL WRITING STYLE

Identify and correct the following stylistic flaws: (ID) inflated diction, (W) wordiness, (J) jargon, (P) passive or passive sense, (A) abstraction, (IT) interrogative trap, (C) cliché, (ABB) excessive abbreviation, (PERS) errors of person. Some sentences will have more than one error and some errors can be identified in different ways. For example, an abstraction may also be a cliché. See the Appendix for answers.

1. It is seen that the train was traveling at excessive speed.
2. C may bring a course of action in negligence against D.
3. The question of liability arises.
4. Can there be any doubt as to the defendant's intent?
5. Sue (S) and Red (R) were both drunk.
6. This country can ill afford such breaches.
7. Since Mr. Kent relies on Blue for all visual perceptions, he was not in imminent apprehension of the act com-

mitted by, or as such was testified to and alleged to have been, committed by Crummy and Nasty.

8. Whereas the above-mentioned, hereinafter referred to as (R) could have interceded, he may have liability.

9. As regards the intentional infliction of emotional distress, it could be observed that a cause of action might lie.

10. Is there any doubt that the defendant should have known what would result from his action?

11. I'm uncertain of the facts regarding the condition of the highway.

12. As the defendant tried to intricate himself from his dilemma, he slipped and fell, subsequently injuring himself.

13. When the train was robbed by the defendants, the opening of the safe was carried out by the Pinkerton men.

14. Def. was eff. prohib. from entering that evid.

15. Mere words regardless of the manner or meaning with which they are verbalized or spoken cannot in any circumstance constitute and/or substantiate an assault.

16. Wouldn't a reasonable person have jumped out of the taxi at such a time?

17. But, in any case involving a discrimination basis for refusal of advancement or employment itself, the facts of that case in particular should have some legal basis to be heard and acted upon.

18. I must advise John to take no action against the six football players because he has no facts that can be shown to have constituted an assault by the six football players.

19. Can there be any other conclusion?

20. When you make another person apprehensive of an immediate battery, that is assault.

21. The law must be able to stand in the light of the truth.

22. The defendant was drinking as it were, and had no recollection of the accident.

23. The penultimate interrogative in this issue concerns proper assessment of liability.

24. An accused layman only slows the process of justice, if justice ever succeeds from the outcome of the case and he will probably end up accepting counsel after he rec-

ognizes that he has failed to convince the court and the people that he is incapable of defending himself.

25. How could the defendant have done anything else?
26. When you bring such an action, you might expect a counterclaim.
27. Ass. and bat. are the two major issues.
28. In order to have an action whose cause lies in intentional infliction of emotional distress, there must be a tortious act which is outrageous and/or beyond the bounds of anything which could be socially approved in today's society pursuant to existing moral codes and structures.
29. When duty is breached in such a fashion as will be hereafter apparent from the discussion infra, A is liable.
30. The R.R. (R) will defend itself on the ground that the train was not operated in interstate commerce.

CHAPTER NINE
Sample Problems and Answers

INTRODUCTION

By the time you get to this chapter, you probably have a good feel for the writing process as it applies to law exams, briefs, and memoranda. In this chapter, we provide a number of sample writing assignments with sample answers. We encourage you to select a problem and write on it as an exercise to improve your writing skills. As you go through the writing process over and over, you will continue to improve your ability to analyze, organize, write, and edit your answers.

After you write your answer to the question, compare it with the sample answer. Remember that the sample answer is not perfect, but that it is a good response to the question. You should go through the entire writing process instead of simply examining the question and reading through the answer. This way, you will have a better understanding of the particular difficulties and twists in each problem and the strategies required to write a successful answer.

CAVEAT

To help students who would like to do all of the problems that follow, we provide "rules" of law with each problem. We must warn you, however, that the rules are vastly oversimplified. If you believe—after reading these rules—that you are knowledgeable about the law in these areas, you may be in for some serious disappointment. We leave teaching law to law professors. All we provide in this chapter are some simplified rules with which to answer our legal writing problems.

PROBLEM ONE: ABNER AND JUDY

Abner and his cousin Judy left the Midwest to take the trip to Metropolis they had planned for so long. Despite their excitement at visiting the big city, they were greatly concerned by the stories of muggings and robberies that were often related to them by friends who had visited there. Consequently, Abner and Judy were more than usually upset when they discovered that their hotel had no record of their reservations and that they had to walk six dark blocks to a neighboring hotel that could accommodate them. After walking only one block, they noticed two men walking behind them and rapidly overtaking them. As Abner looked back nervously, the two men looked away and appeared to have no interest in them. Still, Abner, who was very protective of cousin Judy, became more and more apprehensive.

As the two men overtook Abner and Judy, Abner stopped and pulled Judy out of the way. At that the two men also stopped and turned to face the couple. One said "Hey Buddy . . . ," at which moment Abner, with his souvenir collapsible Metropolitan umbrella, struck the man sharply on the head, knocking him out.

The other man, Frank, a chef who was carrying his favorite boning knife home to sharpen it properly, pulled it from a bag he was carrying and gracefully thrust it into Abner's right shoulder, seriously wounding him.

Judy then brandished her own umbrella, slapping it sharply against her hand for emphasis. The man with the knife turned, broke into a creditable sprint, and disappeared around the corner.

Meanwhile, it began to rain. Concerned about Abner, Judy opened her own umbrella to protect him from the weather until help came. As she opened the umbrella, however, one of the wires supporting the fabric sprang out and struck and injured her right eye.

After the police arrived, they discovered that the man who had been knocked unconscious was Mr. Naybor, a well-known business-man and owner of a nearby restaurant, who claimed he had only been trying to warn the couple to be careful on such dark streets. The other man, Frank, was his head chef. Abner admitted he had made a mistake.

Discuss the following issues:

1. The businessman, Mr. Naybor, wants to sue Abner for battery to recover his medical expenses.
2. Abner wants to sue Frank for battery to recover his medical expenses.
3. Judy, to recover her medical expenses, wants to sue the umbrella manufacturer for manufacturing a defective umbrella.

Assume the following to be valid legal principles:

Battery. A battery is a harmful or offensive touching of an-other that is intentional, unconsented, and unprivileged. However, a person has a privilege to touch another in self-defense as long as he or she does not use any more force than is necessary to prevent an assailant from harming him or her. Furthermore, one has a right to defend oneself even if one makes a reasonable mistake as to the necessity of self defense.

Product Liability. A manufacturer is absolutely liable for any defects in a product that are caused by the manufacturer and not by abuse of the product.

Sample Answer: Abner and Judy

As a result of a misunderstanding and altercation on a dark street in Metropolis, two actions in battery are in question. A pos-sible action in product liability is also indicated.

Naybor v. Abner (Battery). Mr. Naybor, a local businessman, may want to bring an action in battery against Abner, a visitor to the city. Abner, thinking he was about to become the victim of a mugging, struck Mr. Naybor over the head with an umbrella. The question is whether that action constituted a battery.

Battery requires an intentional and harmful or offensive touching. When Abner delivered the blow to Mr. Naybor's head with the umbrella, it was an intentional act that caused harm and was offensive to him. However, a battery must also be unconsented and unprivileged. Although Mr. Naybor did not consent to the blow, Abner may have privilege if he acted in self-defense or even if he made a reasonable mistake as to the necessity of acting in self-defense.

Because Abner was mistaken, the issue is whether the mistake was reasonable. The street was dark, and Abner may have had reason to be nervous about muggers. Naybor himself said he stopped to warn the couple. Still, it is problematic whether Mr. Naybor gave Abner cause to strike him. Mr. Naybor only said "Hey Buddy," a form of address that does not necessarily carry with it a threat, although it isn't particularly cordial. Also, although Naybor and Frank were overtaking Abner and Judy, and they did stop and turn to Abner, Naybor made no other gesture that could be construed as threatening. However, the form of address, the surroundings, and the nature of approach might very well be enough for a reasonable person to think he was about to be mugged.

The next question, however, is whether that reasonable apprehension would be enough to cause a reasonable person to use the amount of force Abner used. Abner may have believed he had to act at that instant or become a victim. However, because he could have spoken to the stranger, and because there was a high probability of error in his assessment of the situation, Abner probably used more force than he had privilege to use. Therefore, because he did not have privilege to strike Mr. Naybor as he did, he should be liable to him for battery.

Abner v. Frank (Battery). After Abner had struck Naybor with the umbrella and knocked him out, Frank stabbed Abner with the boning knife he was carrying in a bag. As a result, Abner wishes to bring an action in battery against Frank, the chef.

It is clear that Frank touched Abner intentionally and harmed him. The question is whether he had any privilege to do so. He may have had privilege if he were acting in self-defense, because one may touch another in self-defense if he or she uses no more force than is necessary.

In this case, the question is whether Frank, by stabbing Abner with a knife, used more force than he had privilege to use. On the one hand, Abner only had an umbrella—a souvenir one at that. Still, it proved effective, as it was sufficient to knock out Mr. Naybor. Also, since it was dark there may be some question as to whether Frank knew what kind of weapon Abner used.

But were there any other options for Frank rather than proceeding directly to potentially deadly force? He could have run away, as he did later, but he would have had to abandon his employer, who was unconscious. He did run away later, but by then the situation had changed, and Abner had been wounded. Frank could also have spoken to Abner to try to see what the situation actually was. But there is no indication that he spoke to Abner. He did react instantly, but was the reaction reasonable?

Because there were other options open to Frank, and because there is no indication that it was necessary at that moment for Frank to use potentially deadly force, it appears that he used more force than he had privilege to use. Therefore, he will be liable to Abner for battery.

Judy v. Umbrella Manufacturer (Product Liability).   Following the stabbing, Judy slapped her own umbrella against her hand as she brandished it. The chef turned and ran. Then she opened her umbrella only to have a wire spring out and injure her eye. As a result, she wishes to bring action against the manufacturer of the umbrella because a manufacturer is absolutely liable for any defects in a product that are caused by the manufacturer and not by abuse of the product.

The first issue is whether Judy abused the umbrella. It is true that she slapped it against her hand for emphasis. We do not know the amount of force she used. It may be argued that because an umbrella is not made to be slapped against the hand or used as a weapon, Judy abused it. However, it is also true that an umbrella should be made to withstand normal wear and tear. A manufacturer should foresee that an umbrella may be tossed into a closet or the trunk of a car, or that it may be tapped on the ground to shake off water. It is hard to tell how hard Judy slapped the umbrella against her hand, but that act in and of itself does not necessarily indicate abuse.

The law requires not only that there be no abuse of the product, but that the defect be caused by the manufacturer. Here is a problem. Not much is known about the umbrella. It is not clear if this too is a souvenir—as is Abner's umbrella. Judy's umbrella's age, condition, or prior use is unknown. There is no indication of a defect specifically caused by the manufacturer.

Because no abuse of the product can be substantiated, and because no specific defect caused by the manufacturer can be ascertained, there can be no finding of liability in this issue without more facts. Based on the facts presented, the manufacturer cannot be found liable.

PROBLEM TWO:
CHRIS THE COCKTAIL WAITRESS

Chris Connors, a cocktail waitress at Earl's Lounge and Restaurant, was walking through the crowded lounge intending to serve a round of drinks when she was touched indelicately by Wilson Smith, one of the customers. She was so startled by the touch that she dropped her tray on the table of a party of four, slightly injuring one member of the party, a law student named Marvin Bailey, and spilling liquor over all of them. Marvin suffered a cut nose.

Marvin, very upset at being injured and also at being forced to hurry home to change his clothes before his evening torts class, went immediately to his car and backed directly into a car driven by Dean Gruff. Both automobiles were damaged.

Meanwhile, Chris retrieved the dropped tray, cleaned up around the table, brought new drinks, and, on her way back to the bar, took the tray and delivered a convincing blow to the top of Wilson Smith's head. Smith was surprised and offended, because, given the nature of Chris's job and her brief uniform, he assumed she could handle the overt behavior he considered to be appropriate to bar atmosphere.

Discuss the following issues:

1. Chris Connors wants to sue Wilson Smith for battery.
2. Marvin Bailey wants to sue Wilson Smith for Bailey's injury, his cleaning bill, and for repair to his own and Dean Gruff's car, all as a result of battery.
3. Wilson Smith wants to sue Chris Connors for battery.

Assume the following to be valid legal principles:

A battery is a harmful or offensive touching of another that is intentional, unconsented, and unprivileged. However, one may have a privilege to touch another in self-defense as long as he or she does not use any more force than is necessary to prevent an assailant from harming him or her. Furthermore, one has a right to defend oneself, even if one makes a reasonable mistake as to the necessity of self defense.

(Further clarification of intent: If a defendant intends to touch one person, and in the process causes another to be touched, the wrongful intent is transferred to the unintended victim. The defendant will then be liable for resulting damages as long as those results should be foreseeable and as long as there is no intervening cause for those results.)

Sample Answer: Chris the Cocktail Waitress

A number of actions in battery result from an incident at a crowded cocktail lounge.

Chris Connors v. Wilson Smith (Battery).   Chris Connors, a cocktail waitress at Earl's Lounge and Restaurant, wishes to bring an action in battery against Wilson Smith, one of the customers. While serving drinks, Chris was touched indelicately by Smith. For there to be liability, the touch must have been intentional, unprivileged, unconsented, and harmful or offensive.

The first question is whether it was intentional. The facts do not state explicitly that Smith touched her intentionally. His later comments, however, in which he characterizes the touch as "overt behavior" he thought she could "handle," and describing it as "appropriate," demonstrate that it was an intentional touch.

There is no legal privilege indicated, but Smith suggests that there was consent. Though Chris did not give verbal consent, Smith suggests that she implied her consent to be touched indelicately by her brief costume and by the nature of her job as a cocktail waitress.

Even though Smith considered his behavior to be appropriate under these conditions, it is questionable whether a reasonable person would confirm his assumptions. First, the brief costume Chris wore on her job would no more be an invitation to touch than a swimming suit at a beach or shorts at a shopping mall. Her manner of dress, then, would not suggest an implied consent to touching.

The nature of Chris's job is to serve drinks. It may be argued that she should expect patrons to have lower inhibitions. Even so, because there is no indication that Smith's actions were customary in the bar or that there was any other invitation from Chris, a reasonable person would not assume that Chris had consented to an indelicate touch.

Finally, although Chris was not physically injured, she would point out that the touch was offensive. Smith might argue that she overreacted and that a reasonable cocktail waitress would not have taken offense. But an unwelcome indelicate touch would embarrass, anger, and offend any reasonable person.

Therefore, because all of the elements of battery are present, Smith will be liable to Chris Connors for battery.

Bailey v. Smith (Battery). Marvin Bailey, a customer at Earl's, also wishes to bring an action in battery against Wilson Smith. When Smith touched and startled Chris, she dropped a tray of drinks on Bailey and his party, soiling his clothes and cutting his nose. After this incident, he also left in a hurry and had an auto accident in the parking lot.

The first element in question is intent. Smith will point out that he did not intend for Bailey to be touched and that he meant no harm to anyone. However, the law says that when one intends to touch one person and in the process causes another to be touched, the wrongful intent is transferred to the unintended victim. That is just what happened in this case. Smith intended to touch Chris and in the process caused Bailey to be touched. He will therefore be liable for all damages as long as those damages are foreseeable and there is no intervening cause.

First, the incident in the lounge must be considered. Smith's touch did cause the drinks to be spilled. There was no intervening cause. Were those results, however, foreseeable? Smith will argue that they were not, and that he had no way of knowing that he might cause damage to another customer. But Chris was carrying a tray of drinks. A reasonable person should know that by startling her with an indelicate touch she might very well spill those drinks and drop the tray. Furthermore, the bar was crowded. If she dropped her tray, it is foreseeable that it might strike another customer.

Because the results should have been foreseeable, and because there was no other cause, Smith should be liable for the damages inside the bar.

The incident in the parking lot is another question. Was it foreseeable? Because it was removed in time and distance from Smith's act, it would be difficult to claim that it should have been foreseeable.

A more specific defense, however, would be intervening cause. The direct cause of the accident appears to be Marvin's own lack of due care rather than Smith's touch. In any case, because Smith did not cause the accident and there was an intervening cause, Wilson Smith will not be liable for the damages sustained in the parking lot.

Smith v. Chris (Battery).   Wilson Smith wishes to bring an action in battery against Chris Connors. Some time following the touching incident, Chris delivered a blow to Smith's head with her tray. The blow was harmful, intentional, and unconsented; the question is whether there was any privilege on Chris's part.

Chris may claim she acted in self-defense. One has the right to act in self-defense so long as one uses no more force than necessary. First, was she acting in self-defense? Although Chris may claim she had to prevent Smith from touching her again and was responding to his touch, there is a question about the time lapse involved. Chris had time to clean up around the table, go to the bar, order new drinks, serve them, and only then did she strike Smith. It seems more likely that the blow was retaliatory rather than defensive.

Was the blow a result of a reasonable mistake about the necessity of self-defense? Chris may have thought she had to do something to dissuade Smith from additional touches. Although there is no indication that he planned to touch her again, his comments about the appropriateness of his action were made even after the touch.

Even if she were acting in self-defense, however, she could use no more force than necessary to prevent an assailant from harming her. Was a blow with a tray the only alternative open to her? She could have called the manager or some other employee if she feared for her safety. She could have spoken to Smith, and there is no indication that she did. In any case, because Smith was not offering force that matched the blow Chris delivered, it would appear that Chris used excessive force even if she had a right of self-defense.

Because Chris Connors had no privilege to strike Wilson Smith as she did, she should be liable to him for battery.

PROBLEM THREE: RACHEL WORTH

On a Saturday afternoon, Mrs. Rachel Worth took her grandson, Freddy, to the Gregory Department Store to buy him a new cap. Mrs. Worth was waited on by a Ms. Doolittle, who found an appropriate cap and sold it to her. Mrs. Worth put the cap on Freddy's head in the presence of Ms. Doolittle after removing the old one and putting it in her purse. She then handed Ms. Doolittle a ten dollar bill, and Ms. Doolittle took it to another part of the store to get change. When she returned the change, Mrs. Worth took her grandson to another part of the store so she could look at ladies' tennis shoes.

While Mrs. Worth was browsing, Mrs. Gregory, the owner of the department store, came up to her and said, "Lady, give me whatever you put in your purse. Give me your purse so I can take it out." Mrs. Worth protested that she didn't take anything and that she had bought a cap and had only put the old one in the purse. Mrs. Gregory said, "Give me the purse." She then said that Mrs. Worth could not leave the store. When Mrs. Worth started to leave anyway, Mrs. Gregory grabbed the purse from her hand and dumped out the contents. When Mrs. Gregory started going through the contents, Mrs. Worth was afraid to leave because she knew the owner could plant something in her purse. Mrs. Gregory finally put the cap in a bag and returned the bag and the purse to Mrs. Worth. (Later, Mrs. Gregory explained that one of her employees reported seeing Mrs. Worth putting something in her purse.) But upon returning her belongings, Mrs. Gregory swore at Mrs. Worth and told her never to return to her store. Shaken, Mrs. Worth left but was ill and required medical treatment for her nervous condition.

Mrs. Worth later consulted her attorney, who called Mrs. Gregory. That night Mrs. Worth received several anonymous, obscene, and threatening telephone calls. More such calls were received on the next two nights. Ultimately, the police found that the calls were made by Mrs. Gregory. Unfortunately, by that time Mrs. Worth was so upset that she required psychiatric treatment.

What are Mrs. Worth's rights against Mrs. Gregory?

Assume the following to be valid legal principles:

1. False imprisonment is the intentional physical or psychological confinement of the plaintiff by the defendant, without consent and without legal privilege. Psychological confinement exists when the plaintiff is placed under no physical restraint but submits to a threat of force or asserted legal authority.

   A shopkeeper has a right to detain for investigation only when there has been an apparent wrongful taking and where the detention and investigation are carried out promptly and in a reasonable manner.

2. Intentional infliction of mental distress consists of conduct of an outrageous nature on the part of the defendant that is calculated to cause and does cause the plaintiff severe mental or emotional distress.

Sample Answer: Rachel Worth

A suspected shoplifting incident in a department store presents issues of false imprisonment and intentional infliction of mental distress.

Rachel Worth v. Mrs. Gregory (False Imprisonment).   Rachel Worth, a customer shopping in the Gregory Department Store, was stopped by Mrs. Gregory and detained while being accused of shoplifting. As a result, she wishes to bring an action against Mrs. Gregory for false imprisonment. False imprisonment consists of an intentional physical or psychological confinement of the plaintiff by the defendant without consent and without legal privilege.

The first issue is whether Rachel Worth was actually confined at all. It may be argued that she was not physically restrained. She was not held or bound physically, but when she did attempt to leave, Mrs. Gregory grabbed her purse, a physical act. Even if this is not enough to constitute physical confinement, there may have been psychological confinement.

Psychological confinement exists when one submits to a threat of force or asserted legal authority. In this case, Mrs. Gregory, upon confronting Mrs. Worth, stopped her and forcefully demanded her purse. When Rachel Worth protested, Mrs. Gregory told her she could not leave the store. This statement at least carries with it the essence of threat, the point being that she was not free to leave. In addition, under these circumstances—involving an accusation of shoplifting—Mrs. Worth must have been aware that the woman was acting for the store. Later she indicated she was afraid *the owner* would plant something in her purse. So there was in this situation an assertion and an assumption of legal authority.

Furthermore, a key element in a consideration of psychological confinement is the purse itself. Mrs. Gregory may claim that Rachel Worth was free to leave without her purse. But for a woman to forfeit her purse, especially when she believed that something might be "planted" in it, whether that suspicion was with or without merit, would be unreasonable. She cannot be said to have been free to leave when psychologically she was placed in fear of leaving. She was, in fact, psychologically confined.

A similar question of consent may be raised. By staying, did Mrs. Worth consent to her detention? She had already indicated her intention to leave, and in fact tried to leave before Mrs. Gregory grabbed her purse. Although she stayed without being held or bound, it was not of her choice.

The major issue in this case is whether Mrs. Gregory had a legal privilege to confine Mrs. Worth. A shopkeeper has a right to detain for investigation when there is an apparent wrongful taking and where investigation is carried out promptly and in a reasonable manner.

According to Mrs. Gregory, a store employee had told her that she had seen Mrs. Worth putting something in her purse. This in itself does not seem unusual, but apparently the employee thought that it was done in a suspicious manner, as we have no other motive suggested. This report, thin as it was, was probably enough to allow Mrs. Gregory to check it out further.

The question of promptness seems not to be a problem for two reasons. First, Mrs. Gregory went promptly to Rachel Worth to confront her. If anything, this may have been too prompt because she did not check with Ms. Doolittle, the clerk who had waited on Mrs. Worth. Also, the duration of the investigation was not extended. She was not held for hours. In fact, the investigation itself was abrupt and brief.

The real question is whether it was carried out in a reasonable manner. On the one hand, Mrs. Gregory is faced with an uncooperative customer. She has received a report of suspected shoplifting, and Mrs. Worth is not carrying a store bag. If Rachel Worth had showed her the purse and explained, Mrs. Gregory would not have had to resort to grabbing the purse. She will point out that Mrs. Worth tried to leave the store without allowing the search and that she had to react in some way.

Still, Mrs. Gregory must react in a reasonable way. She could have delayed Mrs. Worth by politely asking her to wait in the first place. She could have called for the clerk. With a less confrontational manner, she may have been able to avoid the resulting scene. Her actions of demanding and then grabbing the purse, and then dumping out the contents, seem unreasonable—especially in view of the rather slim and insubstantial nature of the suspicion of wrongdoing. Given all of these facts, the investigation does not seem to have been carried out reasonably, and therefore, Mrs. Gregory's actions do not qualify as legal privilege under a shopkeeper's right to detain.

Worth v. Gregory (Intentional Infliction of Mental Distress). Following the search of Rachel Worth's purse, Mrs. Gregory swore at her and told her never to return to her store. Later, Mrs. Gregory made anonymous, obscene, and threatening telephone calls to Mrs. Worth on three consecutive nights. Rachel Worth wishes to bring an action for intentional infliction of mental distress against Mrs. Gregory. Intentional infliction of mental distress requires that the defendant engage in outrageous conduct that is calculated to cause and that does cause severe mental or emotional distress.

The first question is whether Mrs. Gregory's conduct is outrageous. There is no question that she behaved rudely in the store, both in her detention and in her subsequent swearing at Rachel Worth. Is this enough to be termed outrageous? If there is any question about the nature of that behavior, her subsequent acts of making the anonymous, obscene, and threatening telephone calls leave no such question. The calls were outrageous conduct.

Was this behavior calculated to cause severe mental distress? In the department store, it may be that the grabbing of the purse and the swearing were spontaneous results of frustration and anger. It would be difficult to establish that Mrs. Gregory did that in order to cause Mrs. Worth severe distress. It could, however, be argued that the swearing was done just for that purpose. There is no such question about the telephone calls. A reasonable person would know that obscene and threatening calls would cause severe distress. Because they were placed night after night, the caller must have intended to cause that distress. Thus, at least that particular outrageous conduct was done to cause severe distress.

Finally, did the conduct cause distress enough to be classified as severe? Following the incident at the store, Mrs. Worth was shaken and ill, requiring treatment for her nervous condition. The degree of distress may be in question here, as well as whether her nervousness was part of a pre-existing condition. Her condition following the telephone calls, however, leaves no doubt about the severity. She was so upset as to require psychiatric treatment.

Because Mrs. Gregory's conduct was of an outrageous nature, and because it did result in the severe mental and emotional distress it was calculated to cause, Mrs. Gregory will be liable to Rachel Worth for intentional infliction of mental distress.

CONCLUSION

As you have read through these sample answers, we hope you have paid special attention to the logic and support provided for each conclusion. Each answer is organized by issue, and each issue is discussed one step at a time. Look back at the way facts are *used* and not just included or restated. Apply the IRAC guidelines. You will see that the issue has been clearly stated, the rule has been stated and then applied to the relevant facts, and the discussion has led the reader directly to the conclusion.

As you write your own answers, compare them to the samples. Then, later on, you can write on the exercise questions that follow in the Appendix.

Afterword

In this textbook, we have introduced the reader to the kind of writing required in law school. We have explained just what one must do in writing an answer to a law examination question, a legal memorandum, and a brief. We have also taken the reader, step-by-step, through the recursive writing process, including pre-writing, drafting, and revising.

As we have presented strategies and techniques for writing various law school assignments, we have relied on the process approach to writing. We have explained that, to be successful, students must consider not just the product (the resulting written document), but also the pre-writing analysis and organization; the substantive, stylistic, and mechanical concerns during the drafting stage; and the questions for revision presented in Chapter 1.

We have reviewed grammar and style in separate chapters and have urged writers to avoid the highly contagious "legalese." In addition, we have explained the logical constructs involved in legal analysis and argument, and have presented several law examination questions with sample answers.

Throughout this textbook, we have tried to provide a way of approaching a legal writing assignment so that the student will know exactly what is expected and will have strategies for achieving success. We know that what students have learned from this book will help them to be successful in their law school studies. But we have to conclude by urging that writing is a skill that can only be mastered with care and practice. In this book, we have offered an explanation of the task and strategies for success. Mastery will come only with continual and thoughtful application to the task of legal writing.

APPENDIX
Writing Exercises

QUICK WRITES

These first three exercises are short legal problems. Using the facts and law given, write an answer that demonstrates your analysis of the problem and the soundness of your conclusion.

Quick Write 1

A and B robbed a liquor store. A's gun went off accidentally, and the clerk was shot and killed. The robbery was a felony. A state statute holds that when a victim is killed in the commission of a felony, all defendants shall be charged with murder in the first degree.

Discuss the charge of first-degree murder against B.

Quick Write 2

Rodney and Billy were playing war in front of Billy's house. In the course of one battle, Billy threw a rock (hand grenade) at Rodney. Unfortunately, it hit Charles who was passing by on the sidewalk. Charles sustained a serious eye injury and wants to sue Billy for the injury.

Discuss Charles's action against Billy.

Assume the following to be a valid legal principle:

A *battery* is a harmful or offensive touching of another that is intentional, and without consent or legal privilege. *Transfer of intent* exists when one intends a battery against one person and unintentionally causes another person to be harmfully or offensively touched. In that case, the actor is liable to that other person.

Quick Write 3

Huge Hugo, the neighborhood bully, encounters Ronald in an alley. Without moving a muscle, Hugo tells Ronald he is going to jump on Ronald's head. With that Hugo smiles, but not in a friendly way. Ronald leaves immediately and becomes sick from fear. Later he wants to bring an action for assault against Hugo.

Discuss Ronald's action for assault.

Assume the following to be a valid legal principle:

Assault is an intentional, unprivileged, unconsented act that causes reasonable apprehension of an immediate battery. Words alone do not constitute an assault. A threatening gesture must accompany the words.

LEGAL WRITING QUESTIONS

The following writing exercises present facts, law, and legal issues. Use them to practice writing thoughtful, complete, and clear analytical answers. You may use the rules of law provided, or you may rely on your own knowledge of law.

Writing Exercise 1: Charlie and Jack

Charlie was a local weight lifter and bully who liked to start fights. Although quite strong, he was extremely slow moving, and he limited himself to brawling with people who were considerably smaller than he.

Jack was a small, unathletic man who confined his exercise to daily jogging and attempts to stuff himself with enough food to boost his weight over 115 pounds. Unfortunately, he frequented the same bar as Charlie (a place called the Dew Drop Inn). One day while Jack was drinking a high-calorie banana daiquiri, Charlie lumbered over wearing a malicious grin. "You're next, Jackie-boy," he said. "Next time I see you it's going to be all over."

Jack left immediately and thereafter began carrying a gun every time he left his house. Three nights later, while taking a short-cut through an alley, he saw a huge figure about thirty yards away lumbering slowly toward him. Because the figure was about the same size as Charlie, Jack became frightened, drew his gun, and fired. Then he ran home.

Jack's shot grazed Fred, a construction worker who was cutting through the alley on his way home. He now sues Jack for battery. What result?

Assume the following to be valid legal principles:

A *battery* is the harmful or offensive touching of another that is intentional, unconsented, and unprivileged. However, a person may touch another in self-defense as long as he or she does not use any more force than is necessary to prevent an assailant from harming him or her. Furthermore, one has a right (privilege) to defend oneself even if one makes a *reasonable* mistake as to the necessity of self-defense.

Writing Exercise 2: Red and Sue

Red, a Los Angeles resident, and his girlfriend, Sue, also a Los Angeles resident, decide to drive to Las Vegas for the weekend in Red's new Cadillac. They stop in Barstow, California, pick up a bottle of Old Tennis Shoe Rye Whiskey, and proceed to drink and drive on their way. As they travel at high speed in their erratic trip across the Nevada desert, Sue, a little drunk, decides her skill at steering the car is better than Red's and playfully grabs the steering wheel. The car swerves sharply, the left front wheel comes off, and the Cadillac crashes into a cactus, injuring both Red and Sue.

Discuss the possible law suits resulting from this accident.

Assume the following to be valid legal principles:

—According to Nevada and California law, suits resulting from this accident may be brought in either state.
—Both California and Nevada hold drinking while driving to be negligent. Negligence implies liability.
—If one does not exercise due care and causes another's injury, that person is deemed negligent and is liable for the other's injury.
—If one does not exercise due care and contributes to one's own injury, that person is deemed contributorily negligent. Contributory negligence is a defense to an action in negligence. Recovery is diminished according to the amount of fault in causing the injury.
—Both states stipulate that a manufacturer is responsible for any damages resulting from defective parts.

Writing Exercise 3: Durwood

Durwood was burglarizing a house when he heard some noises upstairs. He grabbed a poker from the fireplace and hid behind a curtain. Looking up at the stairs, he saw someone's foot on the top step. "Don't take another step," he shouted. "If you come out here I'll kill you." The person at the top of the steps froze, and Durwood slipped out of the window. Durwood has been captured by the police.

Assume that you have been told these facts by your boss, the district attorney, and that she has asked you to write her a memo in which you tell her whether to charge first- or second-degree burglary. She will be out of town while you are writing this memo, so you will have to give her alternative courses of action if you don't have enough facts.

Assume the following statutes are in effect in your jurisdiction:

Section 460. Degrees: Every burglary of an inhabited dwelling-house committed in the nighttime, and every burglary of an inhabited dwelling house, whether in the daytime or nighttime, committed by a person armed with a deadly weapon, or who while in the commission of such burglary arms himself with a deadly weapon, or who while in the commission of such burglary assaults any person, is burglary of the first degree. All other kinds of burglary are of the second degree.

Section 240. Assault: A criminal assault is an unlawful attempt, coupled with a present ability, to commit a violent injury on the person of another.

Writing Exercise 4: Roman Round

Roman Round, a traveling salesman with districts in the states of Glacier and Forest, married his childhood sweetheart, Susan, in a civil ceremony in Glacier in 1955. In 1962 twin daughters, Annie and Fannie, were born to them. Roman, however, had a girlfriend named Alice who also lived in Glacier. Alice had a son, Homer, by Roman in 1962. Susan died in 1963, at which time Roman moved in with Alice. They lived together as husband and wife, and in 1973 had another child, Rupert. In addition, they adopted a seventeen-year-old girl named Ruby in 1974. In 1971 Roman had met and married Nora in Forest. He lived with her when in Forest and with Alice when in Glacier. Roman and Nora had a child, Fred, in 1972.

Roman attended a sales convention in Atlantic City in 1994, at which time, while swimming with Rita, a cocktail waitress, he was devoured by a shark. Rita was not injured. Roman left no will, but did leave an estate of $100,000.

Discuss the inheritance rights of all the parties.

Assume the rules in this jurisdiction are as follows:

—When there is no will, both the states of Glacier and Forest divide property equally among the decedent's living legal wife and legitimate children.

—Marriage at common law in both states is valid after seven years of cohabitation.

—Legitimate children are children born of any valid marriages.

—An adopted child is also a legitimate child.

—Bigamy, entering into a marriage while already married, is illegal, and all marriages subsequent to the valid one are void.

Writing Exercise 5: Sam the Swimmer

Sam, a Muscle Beach regular, was swimming about a hundred yards off shore in the early afternoon of a cold fall day. The beach was deserted this day except for two people, Donna and Harold. Sam got a cramp and began thrashing around, calling for help and yelling that he was drowning. Harold, an off-duty, trained lifeguard, urged Donna to stay on the beach because of her cold and sore throat, in spite of the fact that she was an Olympic swimmer. Harold then swam out to help the drowning man. When Harold reached the swimmer and saw that it was Sam, a reviled enemy, he executed a smooth turn and headed back to shore. Sam went down for the third time. Donna was hysterical and later had to be hospitalized because she knew that she could have saved Sam.

Discuss the suits resulting from this incident.

Assume the following to be valid legal principles:

There is no affirmative duty to go to the aid of another. If one does go to the aid of another, the rescuer is under an obligation not to place the victim in any worse position than he or she was in before.

Writing Exercise 6: George and Mabel

George and Mabel, on a visit to the city of Saint Frank, buy a ticket for a ride on the city-owned streetcar. They then relax and enjoy the ride as C. Jones, the operator, runs the streetcar and points out the sights. Meanwhile, Ms. Fox, out shopping, had parked her Audi on the tracks, assuming them to be abandoned because no sign was posted indicating they were in service. C. Jones, coming around a curve, saw Ms. Fox's automobile and was barely able to bring the streetcar to a jolting halt before it could strike the car. Mabel and George were both thrown from the streetcar and injured. Mr. Smith, a fellow passenger, jumped from the streetcar to aid George and Mabel, and broke his leg.

Discuss the law suits that may result from this accident.

Assume the following to be valid legal principles:

—The owner of a vehicle parked within five feet of streetcar tracks currently in service is liable for all injuries resulting therefrom.
—One is not required to come to the aid of another, but if he or she does, he or she does so at his or her own risk; that is, he or she cannot recover from the person he or she aided for any injuries he or she may sustain.
—The city is responsible for any injuries resulting from careless or hazardous operation of its streetcar line.

Writing Exercise 7: Budd and Heather

Budd and Heather are sailing on Lake Titan in their boat, *Risky Business,* on a clear day in April. Suddenly a violent mountain storm pushes in and Budd and Heather are forced to find a place to tie up. They spot a private dock owned by a Mr. Vere. Already tied up to the dock is Mr. Vere's thirty-five-foot yacht, *Bellipotent.* Budd and Heather secure the bow of their boat to the *Bellipotent* (because that is the most secure mooring they can achieve) and go below to drink rum and wait out the storm. While Budd and Heather are asleep, their boat is violently knocking against Mr. Vere's yacht, finally battering a hole in it. Mr. Vere, coming upon the scene, shouts at Budd and Heather, waking them up, and demands that they leave. When they refuse to do so, Mr. Vere cuts *Risky Business* loose. It capsizes immediately after that and Heather drowns. Budd swims ashore and is hospitalized with pneumonia. Mr. Vere's yacht is damaged in the amount of $30,000.

Discuss the rights and liabilities of Budd, Heather, and Vere.

Assume the rules in this jurisdiction are as follows:

—The owner of property has a right to use force to eject people who are there without his or her permission, unless he or she knows he or she would thereby cause their death.
—A person is privileged to go upon the property of another to save his or her own life, but he or she accepts the responsibility for being on that property.

Writing Exercise 8: Jones and Green

Jones orally promised to will his home and property to Green if Green took care of Jones's sister, who lived in Sacramento. Green then moved from San Francisco to Sacramento (a distance of eighty miles), where he acted as a domestic servant, attended to Jones's sister's personal needs, and acted as her nurse until her death five years later. When Green informed Jones of his sister's death, Jones suffered a fatal heart attack, leaving a perfectly valid will that gives all of his property to Thompson.

Green comes to you for legal advice. He tells you that he forsook most of his friends and personal pleasures and gave up other lucrative employment opportunities for this job. He wants to know if he is entitled to the home and property.

Assume the rules in this jurisdiction are as follows:

—A will may be revoked at any time before the person who made it dies.

—When a person gives up something of value in reliance upon the promise of another, that person can recover the fair value of what was given up.

—The estate of a deceased person is liable for all of the legitimate debts of that deceased person.

—Any contract to make a will must be in writing or it will not be enforced.

Writing Exercise 9: Baker and Abba

Jim Baker, a seventeen-year-old, five-foot-nine-inch, 139-pound boy, was hitchhiking one afternoon in July. Tom Abba, a heavyset, thirty-five-year-old man, stopped to give him a lift. While driving together, Tom learned that Jim was carrying five thousand dollars to make a drug purchase. Tom stopped the car and suggested that Jim get out, so they both could go for a swim. Both men left the car. Tom pulled a knife and said, "Jim, give me the money." After Jim had handed him the money, Tom said, "I guess I can't leave a witness," and proceeded toward Jim. Jim drew a pistol from under his shirt and fatally shot Tom. Jim has been charged with murder.

Discuss whether Jim is guilty of murder under these facts.

Assume the rules in this jurisdiction are as follows:

—If a person is threatened with deadly force, that person
  has a duty to retreat before employing self-defense.
—There is no duty to retreat where one cannot do so in
  safety.
—If a person kills another in self-defense, that person is not
  guilty of murder.

Writing Exercise 10: Mary Ann Jones

Mary Ann Jones, a woman of about fifty years of age, was
walking down a side street of San Juan, a metropolitan U.S. city,
when she saw a man leaning against the wall about a quarter of a
block away. It was midday and there was traffic on the street, so she
felt it was safe to continue—though she didn't like the unkempt
looks of the man.

As she passed, the man grabbed her purse sharply, breaking
the strap, and staggering Mary Jones as he pulled it from her. He
then broke into a sprint down the sidewalk.

Mary screamed for help.

Steven Brown happened to be driving his cab on that street
and witnessed the incident. He sped after the man, honking his
horn and shouting out of his window.

The man gave no indication he was going to stop. Brown drove
ahead, then swerved and swung his taxi into the man, pinning him
against the wall. Brown jumped from the cab and retrieved Mary
Jones's purse. The man, Gene Green, suffered fractures of both
legs. The cab driver summoned police and an ambulance. Green
was arrested and then taken to a hospital for treatment.

Several weeks later, Green retained an attorney and brought
action in battery against Steven Brown, the cab driver.

Discuss the rights and liabilities of all the parties.

Assume the following to be valid legal principles:

—A *battery* is a harmful or offensive touching of another
  that is intentional, and without consent or legal privilege.
—A defense to battery is the privilege of legal authority. A
  private person may arrest for a crime when (1) the crime

has in fact been committed, and (2) the private person reasonably believes that the arrested person has committed it. Furthermore, a private person making a legal arrest may use only reasonable and necessary force to take the person into custody.

Writing Exercise 11: Mr. Kent

Mr. Kent, an avid astronomer, was watching a solar eclipse without any protection for his eyes. As a result, he became totally blind. To facilitate his normal routine, Mr. Kent undertook a prescribed course on how to use a Seeing Eye dog. After successful completion of the course, he was given a dog named Blue.

While taking his daily walk through Central Park, Mr. Kent noticed that Blue was getting excited. Blue stopped and started growling. Mr. Kent became worried. Two thugs, Crummy and Nasty, were standing there. They spoke harshly to Mr. Kent. Then, for a practical joke, Crummy grabbed the leash from Mr. Kent and ran off with Blue.

Mr. Kent wandered home, tripping and falling once or twice. Having arrived home, Mr. Kent discovered Blue was there. Although happy to be with Blue again, Mr. Kent comes to your law firm seeking recovery from the two thugs. He tells Mr. Knowit, your senior partner, that he wants to sue Crummy and Nasty for battery.

You are a junior partner in the firm. Mr. Knowit relays the above facts to you and wants you to write a memorandum reviewing all the issues, recommending any possible legal action, and discussing possible outcomes.

Assume the following to be valid legal principles:

—A *battery* is a harmful or offensive touching of another that is intentional, and without consent or legal privilege.

—*Intentional infliction of mental distress* requires outrageous conduct on the part of the defendant that is calculated to cause and does cause the plaintiff severe mental or emotional distress.

Writing Exercise 12: Mrs. Trueblue

Mrs. A. Trueblue and her six-year-old daughter went to dinner at the Blue Wolf Restaurant. The waiter, a surly fellow, asked Mrs.

Trueblue, "Well, whaddaya want?" Taken aback at his insolence, Mrs. Trueblue nevertheless ordered two rare steaks. The order came shortly thereafter, burned to a crisp. When Mrs. Trueblue protested, the waiter shouted, "You old witch, what do you expect when you come to a place like this?" He ranted at Mrs. Trueblue and her daughter for another few minutes and then left. Mrs. Trueblue, angered but not flustered, indignantly started to leave. The manager, thinking she hadn't paid her bill (which she hadn't, because the waiter had taken the dinners back), blocked her way, demanding payment. When she attempted to leave, he grabbed her purse, breaking the strap. Being unwilling to leave her purse, Mrs. Trueblue remained in the restaurant for four hours arguing with the manager. Finally the manager let her go. Mrs. Trueblue's young daughter subsequently became quite ill and was unable to sleep well for several weeks because of the waiter's accusation.

Who is liable to whom, and for what?

Assume the following to be valid legal principles:

—*False imprisonment* is the intentional physical or psychological confinement of the plaintiff by the defendant, without consent and without legal privilege. Psychological confinement exists when the plaintiff is placed under no physical restraint but submits to a threat of force or asserted legal authority.

—A *battery* is a harmful or offensive touching of another that is intentional, and without consent or legal privilege.

—*Intentional infliction of mental distress* requires outrageous conduct on the part of the defendant that is calculated to cause and does cause the plaintiff severe mental or emotional distress.

Writing Exercise 13: Eel O'Brien

Although financially down on his luck, Eel O'Brien remained undaunted in his devotion to *Plastic Man* comic books. Unable to afford the slight coinage necessary for procuring the monthly issues, Eel had taken to perusing them at the racks of some of the local drug and grocery stores. Soon, however, having worn out his welcome at these establishments, he ventured onto new territory, Gargantua's Groceries, a dump if ever there was one, with not a soul in sight. Eel enjoyed as best he could the latest exploits of his hero. He then replaced the comic book in the rack and quickly proceeded to the exit, where he encountered Gargantua himself, who, in height, girth, and musculature, seemed a more or less human equivalent of King Kong. Gargantua's body was pressed against the door, removing the exit from sight.

"Gimme it," Gargantua demanded.

"G-g-give you what?" queried Eel, uneasily.

"Unless you take that comic book from under your coat, you're not walking out of here."

Eel, now nearly hysterical with fright, thought he heard an emphasis on "walking" and assumed it meant that his legs were in danger of being broken. Quickly glancing around the store, he saw a back door and sped to it. Gargantua lumbered after, hurling a gallon jug of cranberry juice that missed Eel but struck a Campbell soup display, a can of which rolled under Eel's feet, nearly causing him to trip as he made his way to the rear of the store and out.

Eel has just stormed into your office, wildly recounting these details and shrieking, "Do something, do something!" What, legally, can you do for him?

Assume the following to be valid legal principles:

—*Assault* is an intentional, unprivileged, unconsented act that causes reasonable apprehension of an immediate battery. Words alone do not constitute an assault. A threatening gesture must accompany the words.

—*Intentional infliction of mental distress* requires outrageous conduct on the part of the defendant that is calculated to cause and does cause the plaintiff severe mental or emotional distress.

Writing Exercise 14: Nomad Family

It was moving day for the Nomad family. The Go-Our-Way Transfer Company, scheduled to arrive about 9 a.m., showed up at the Nomad home at about 1 p.m. Because of the late start, it was rather dark when the final item of household goods was loaded on the van. After putting that item on the van, the driver of the transfer truck closed the doors to the van, and then he and his assistant went into the Nomad home to ask Mr. Nomad to sign some papers. While in the house they could not resist, despite company rules to the contrary, Nomad's invitation to have a beer. After all, it had been a long, hot day.

The driver and his helper returned to the truck after an interval of about thirty minutes. As they approached it, they thought they heard a child crying inside the van. Sure enough, upon opening the van doors, they found inside four-year-old Alvin, a child belonging to the neighbors of the Nomads. Little Alvin had been watching the loading most of the afternoon, but this was the first either the driver or helper knew he had been inside the van. When discovered, Alvin was hysterical—obviously frightened and distraught.

As Alvin began screaming, the driver grabbed him while his assistant reclosed the door of the van so they could calm the child. Seeing that Alvin wasn't cooperating with the driver, the assistant raised his hand and said, "Shut up, you brat, or I'll whop you one up alongside the head!" Alvin stopped crying. The two employees then opened the van and allowed Alvin to leave. Alvin then ran home and told his parents. For the next few days Alvin suffered fear of darkness and, when in a closed room, frequently wet his pants. Alvin's parents consult you, an attorney, and ask you to advise them of their rights.

Discuss the rights and liabilities of all the parties involved.

Assume the following to be valid legal principles:

—*Negligence* requires that defendant owe a duty of care to plaintiff and that a breach of that duty be the proximate cause of a particular injury.

—*Assault* is an intentional, unprivileged, unconsented act that causes reasonable apprehension of an immediate battery. Words alone do not constitute an assault. A threatening gesture must accompany the words.

—A *battery* is a harmful or offensive touching of another that is intentional, and without consent or legal privilege.

—*False imprisonment* is the intentional physical or psychological confinement of the plaintiff by the defendant, without consent and without legal privilege.

Key to Exercise, Chapter 7

1. RO
2. AP
3. P
4. SV & SC
5. SV
6. F
7. AM
8. F & SC
9. SV
10. F
11. AP
12. F
13. SV
14. AM
15. F
16. F
17. AM
18. F
19. AM
20. AP
21. AM
22. AM & AP
23. F
24. AM
25. AP
26. F

Key to Exercise, Chapter 8

1. P
2. J
3. P
4. IT
5. No error
6. C & A
7. ID & W
8. W & J
9. W & P
10. IT
11. PERS & W
12. ID
13. P
14. ABB
15. W & J & ID
16. IT
17. A & W & ID
18. W & PERS
19. IT
20. PERS
21. A & C
22. W & C
23. ID & W
24. W
25. IT
26. PERS
27. ABB
28. W & ID
29. J & W
30. ABB

Glossary
of Legal Terms

This glossary is not intended to replace a law dictionary. In compiling it, our intention was to provide a quick reference for technical terms that appear in the text, especially for the use of students who are not in law school. To make terms understandable, we have sometimes had to stretch the technical meaning of a term or to be rather general. If this glossary is used only as a supplement to the text, the looseness of our definitions should not cause any problems. However, we would hate to be quoted when you argue before the United States Supreme Court.

Accomplice   One who is knowingly involved with another in the commission of a crime and therefore shares the guilt. The term is used only when talking about criminal matters.

Action   A catchall term that indicates a proceeding in a court to enforce one's rights. To "begin an action" is to file (with a court) the first papers necessary to start a lawsuit. A person is said to "have an action " or have a "cause of action" (see below) when the facts he or she claims would, if proven, show a violation of rights that the law recognizes. For instance, if one person has hit another, the person who was hit might have a cause of action in battery.

Actionable   Giving grounds to bring an action. For instance, a punch in the nose might be *actionable.*

Adversary   The person who is on the other side of a lawsuit. Where there are two sides in an action it is called an "adversary proceeding." The lawyer for the person bringing the lawsuit would call the lawyer for the person against whom the lawsuit is being brought an *adversary.* Lawyers have been known to use many other names for their opponent, but most of them would not be appropriate for a textbook.

Allegation   A statement by one of the parties to a lawsuit which that party intends to prove. For instance, a person might make the *allegation* that on a certain date and in a certain place another person hit him or her.

Appellant   The person who is unhappy with a decision and takes it to the next higher court asking that it be reversed.

Appellee   The person who is happy with the decision and is dragged kicking and screaming to the next higher court asking that the decision of the lower court be left alone.

Assault   In general, the intentional, unlawful offer to touch another, without his or her consent, thereby placing the other in apprehension of an imminent battery.

Assumption of the risk   A phrase used in negligence law that indicates that a person knew the dangers involved in an activity and took part in that activity. Consequently, the person is prevented from later complaining about an injury received because of those dangers. For instance, a person who goes ice skating *assumes the risk* of sliding on the ice and falling.

Authority   The term refers to an earlier decision that must be followed by a later court. It also means that a person has the legal right to compel an act. For instance, a police officer has the authority to demand to see your driver's license if you are stopped while driving.

Battery   In general, a harmful or offensive touching of another that is intentional, unprivileged, and unconsented.

Breach of peace   Creating a public disturbance. For instance, starting a fist fight in the local tavern might be a *breach of the peace.*

Brief   A researched, written document that argues a client's position to a court. It is an advocacy document intended to persuade.

Briefing   The process of extracting the key elements from a case to understand a court's reason for ruling the way it did.

Burglary   Although the specific crime is defined by laws in most states, in general terms it is the breaking and entering of the dwelling house of another, in the nighttime, with the intention of committing a felony therein.

Case   A lawsuit. A person is often said to "have a case" when there is a chance that the facts alleged, if proven, will result in his or her winning a lawsuit. To brief a case is to take notes on a particular decision.

Case brief, "brief"   The written notes made during the process of briefing are called a "case brief," sometimes shortened to "brief." The word "brief," when used in this way, does *not* refer to an advocacy document, but to an objective document.

Cause of action   Similar to case. Usually, a person is said to have a *cause of action* "in" a particular area. For instance, a person hit by another might have a *cause of action* in battery.

Civil action   An action that seeks redress for personal rights, as opposed to a criminal action.

Community property   Property that is owned together by a husband and wife. If the marital relationship is ended, each party is generally entitled to one-half of all the *community property.*

Complaint   In a civil action it is generally the first set of papers filed. It puts forth the allegations that form the basis for the action.

In a criminal action it is a charge that a certain person has committed a specific crime.

Criminal action   An action brought by the state against a person accused of a public offense. It differs from a civil action in that the state itself is a party.

Defamation   Injuring the reputation of another person, either through a written or an oral statement.

Defendant   The person against whom a lawsuit is brought. (See plaintiff, below.)

Defense   The facts and reasons presented by the defendant as to why the plaintiff should not win the lawsuit. For instance, in a criminal action the accused might allege as a defense that he or she was in another city at the time the crime was committed.

Degree   Classification. Crimes are sometimes divided into different *degrees* as an indication of the relative seriousness with which they are viewed. For instance, there is first-degree and second-degree murder.

Elements of a cause of action   Those acts or omissions that make up the *prima facie* case for a given civil or criminal action.

False imprisonment   In general, depriving another of his or her liberty without legal cause.

Felony   A crime of a serious nature. Murder is an example of a *felony*. A misdemeanor is a crime of a less serious nature.

File an action   To begin a lawsuit by formally presenting the proper papers to the proper court.

Immaterial facts   Those facts that have no relevance to the question being asked. For instance, if the question is whether Smith signed a certain document, the fact that he had his fingers crossed while doing so is *immaterial*.

Indeterminate sentence A prison sentence whose termination date is uncertain at the time that the sentence is originally meted out by the judge. Theoretically, the actual termination date is set by an impartial group on the basis of the prisoner's response to confinement.

Infra Either "within" or "below." In legal writing it is usually used to indicate that something will be more fully described at a later point in the text.

Intentional infliction of mental distress An intentional tort. It requires outrageous conduct on the part of the defendant that is calculated to cause and does cause the plaintiff severe mental or emotional distress.

Invasion of privacy The infringement by one person or agency on another person's legally protected right to be left alone.

Issue The specific legal question that must be decided in a given case. An *issue* can be phrased broadly or narrowly. For instance, the issue in a case could be "whether Mary committed a battery upon John," or it could be "whether John consented to Mary's kissing him on the cheek." In the first formulation the issue is phrased broadly; in the second, narrowly.

Judgment n.o.v. The abbreviation is of the Latin *non obstante veredicto*, which means "notwithstanding the verdict." It is possible for a jury to decide one way in a case and the judge to rule the opposite way. Thus, although the jury believes that one party should be the winner, the judge determines that the other party should win. The judge is then said to have awarded a *judgment n.o.v.*

Jurisdiction The term is comprehensive and not susceptible to quick definition. Naturally, that doesn't deter us. As we have used the term in the text, it refers to whether or not a court has the authority to hear a particular kind of case. For instance, a United States Tax Court could not hear a battery case.

Jurisprudence The philosophy of law.

Legal doctrine   A theory that is used in answering legal questions. For instance, assumption of the risk is a *legal doctrine.*

Legal ethics   A body of moral precepts for the behavior of lawyers. They are codified in the American Bar Association's *Code of Professional Responsibility.*

Legal principle   We have used this term interchangeably with legal doctrine.

Liability   A responsibility that is enforceable in a court of law. For instance, if the question were whether John had any *liability* for Michael's injury, we would be asking whether Michael could force John, through a court action, to pay for his injuries.

Libel   A written defamation.

Material facts   Those facts essential to the determination of a legal issue. They are the opposite of immaterial facts. For instance, whether John gave Mary permission to kiss him would be a *material fact* in a battery action brought by John.

Memorandum   A researched, written answer to one or more legal questions. Often called an "office memo" or "memo," it is an objective document that fairly portrays authorities that are both favorable and unfavorable to your client's position.

Memorandum of points and authorities   A researched, written document that is presented to a court in support of a motion. It is an advocacy document that provides the court with arguments and authorities for deciding the motion in favor of your client.

Negligence   A failure to exercise that degree of care for other people that society expects of individuals. For such a failure one may have liability for damages.

Paralegal   As we have used the term, it refers to one who is specially trained to assist a lawyer and his or her clients in the resolution of legal problems. Generally, a *paralegal* works under the supervision of a *lawyer.*

Plaintiff The person who initiates a lawsuit. In criminal actions, the *plaintiff* is always the state.

Plea bargaining The negotiations between the prosecutor and the defense lawyer in a criminal action. Through this process the defendant may be allowed to plead guilty to a lesser crime so that the prosecution will not have to prove guilt to a court.

Prima facie case A party is said to have a *prima facie case* when the facts he or she has presented, if true, are sufficient to establish his or her cause of action.

Privileged statements Statements that may not be used in a court. For instance, statements a person makes to his or her lawyer when seeking legal advice (with some exceptions) may not be revealed by the lawyer against the client's wishes.

Reasonable person A legal fiction. A hypothetical person against whom the actions of a defendant may be measured. For instance, in a negligence action the question might be whether a *reasonable person* in the defendant's position would have acted in the way in which the defendant acted.

Remedy The legal means through which one obtains redress for a legal wrong. For instance, the *remedy* for a battery might be a lawsuit to recover money as compensation for the physical injury done.

Res ipsa loquitur Literally, the Latin means "the thing speaks for itself." It is a specific legal doctrine in negligence. It is almost invariably misused by students who are attempting to sound like lawyers. It should not be used to replace words like "clearly" or "obviously."

Rights As used in the text, these are expectations one has (such as freedom from interference with one's person) that are protected by the law. It is sometimes said that for every right, there is a remedy.

Robbery In general, the taking of personal property from the possession of another, against his or her will, and through the use of force or fear.

Rule of law A general legal principle that is sufficiently well accepted so that it provides guidance in a doubtful case. It may not be an exact statement of the law in any particular jurisdiction.

Slander A spoken defamation.

Statute A law enacted by a legislative body.

Target crime The primary crime on which other crimes depend. For instance, for there to be a conspiracy to commit robbery, the two people involved would have to commit some acts toward carrying out the robbery. Robbery would be called the *target crime.*

Tort A wrongful act against an individual for which the remedy is a civil action. For instance, battery is a *tort.*

Writ of mandamus An order from a court to a lower court or a public official that commands that court or officials do or not do something that they are legally obliged to do or refrain from doing.

Index